DESTINY
DAILY READINGS

DESTINY
DAILY READINGS
Inspirations for Your Life's Journey

T. D. Jakes

New York   Boston   Nashville

FaithWords
Hachette Book Group
1290 Avenue of the Americas
New York, NY 10104

www.faithwords.com

Printed in the United States of America

RRD-C

First Edition: October 2015
10 9 8 7 6 5 4 3 2

FaithWords is a division of Hachette Book Group, Inc.
The FaithWords name and logo are trademarks of Hachette Book Group, Inc.

The Hachette Speakers Bureau provides a wide range of authors for speaking events. To find out more, go to www.hachettespeakersbureau.com or call (866) 376-6591.

The publisher is not responsible for websites (or their content) that are not owned by the publisher.

Library of Congress Control Number: 2015947596

ISBN 978-1-4555-5395-2 (hardcover) / ISBN – 978-1-4555-6301-2 (ebook)

CONTENTS

xxxxxxxxxxxxxxxxxxxxxxxxxxxx

INTRODUCTION

∞∞∞∞∞∞∞∞∞∞∞∞∞∞∞∞∞∞∞∞∞∞∞

Tamar, Rahab, Ruth, Bathsheba, and Mary were five women who boldly followed their destiny and lived fulfilled and purposeful lives. Each of their daring accounts is told in Scripture, and their stories reveal steps you can take to live your own destiny. Allow these faithful Destiny chasers to serve as your role models as you journey through life wondering where and how you fit in. Use their lives as examples of how—through courage, faith, and persistence—you, too, can reach your destiny and live the life you were created to live.

As you read their stories and glean from the accounts of these five women, remember that not one of them had an easy and pain-free path toward their destiny. In fact, all five of these women had to overcome obstacles and activate faith to reach their destiny. They are the only five women noted in the genealogy in Matthew that lists forty-two generations that led to the birth of Christ. While we know it took both a man and a woman to make each child in the ancestry of Jesus, Bible writers include only the names of these few women among the forty-two men named. What made them stand out? What were their stories? How did their actions contribute to their destiny—to play their part in bringing about God's plan to redeem the world?

Read the daily insights we learn from the five women of the Bible in this book along with my book *Destiny: Step into Purpose* to fully recognize how to live your destiny and enjoy a fulfilling life.

Are you ready to meet your destiny? Are you ready to activate your faith and set out on the path God designed just for you? Are you ready to live on purpose like these women in the lineage of Jesus? Come along for the journey, and prepare to meet your destiny. You can change the world.

T.D. Jakes

Tamar's Story

Genesis 38:6, 11–30 (NIV)

Judah got a wife for Er, his firstborn, and her name was Tamar…

Judah then said to his daughter-in-law Tamar, "Live as a widow in your father's household until my son Shelah grows up." For he thought, "He may die too, just like his brothers." So Tamar went to live in her father's household.

After a long time Judah's wife, the daughter of Shua, died. When Judah had recovered from his grief, he went up to Timnah, to the men who were shearing his sheep, and his friend Hirah the Adullamite went with him.

When Tamar was told, "Your father-in-law is on his way to Timnah to shear his sheep," she took off her widow's clothes, covered herself with a veil to disguise herself, and then sat down at the entrance to Enaim, which is on the road to Timnah. For she saw that, though Shelah had now grown up, she had not been given to him as his wife.

When Judah saw her, he thought she was a prostitute, for she had covered her face. Not realizing that she was his daughter-in-law, he went over to her by the road-side and said, "Come now, let me sleep with you."

"And what will you give me to sleep with you?" she asked.

"I'll send you a young goat from my flock," he said.

"Will you give me something as a pledge until you send it?" she asked.

He said, "What pledge should I give you?"

"Your seal and its cord, and the staff in your hand," she answered. So he gave them to her and slept with her, and she became pregnant by him. After she left, she took off her veil and put on her widow's clothes again.

Meanwhile Judah sent the young goat by his friend the Adullamite in order to get his pledge back from the woman, but he did not find her. He asked the men who lived there, "Where is the shrine prostitute who was beside the road at Enaim?"

"There hasn't been any shrine prostitute here," they said.

So he went back to Judah and said, "I didn't find her. Besides, the men who lived there said, 'There hasn't been any shrine prostitute here.'"

Then Judah said, "Let her keep what she has, or we will become a laughingstock. After all, I did send her this young goat, but you didn't find her."

About three months later Judah was told, "Your daughter-in-law Tamar is guilty of prostitution, and as a result she is now pregnant."

Judah said, "Bring her out and have her burned to death!"

As she was being brought out, she sent a message to her father-in-law. "I am pregnant by the man who owns these," she said. And she added, "See if you recognize whose seal and cord and staff these are."

Judah recognized them and said, "She is more righteous than I, since I wouldn't give her to my son Shelah." And he did not sleep with her again.

When the time came for her to give birth, there were twin boys in her womb. As she was giving birth, one of them put out his hand; so the midwife took a scarlet thread and tied it on his wrist and said, "This one came out first." But when he drew back his hand, his brother came out, and she said, "So this is how you have broken out!" And he was named Perez. Then his brother, who had the scarlet thread on his wrist, came out. And he was named Zerah.

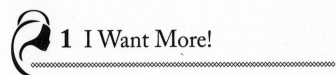 1 I Want More!

This is the genealogy of Jesus the Messiah the son of David, the son of Abraham:.... Judah the father of Perez and Zerah, whose mother was Tamar.

Matthew 1:1, 3 (NIV)

I am Tamar, the first woman mentioned in the lineage of Jesus in Matthew 1. You find my story in Genesis 38. Take some time and read about me, but be forewarned: my story is a messy one. It's not rated G or even PG. It's downright ugly. That's how life can be sometimes; but ugly circumstances don't have to keep you from your destiny.

I married Judah's son Er. He was my first husband, and he died. His death was a consequence of his evil. Then, I married his brother, Onan. That was the custom at the time. If a man died, his brother married the dead brother's widow. It was a way to make sure the deceased man had an heir. But Onan didn't want to produce a child with me; he knew it would be considered his brother's heir. God didn't like Onan's actions, and as a result, Onan died, too. My father-in-law Judah told me to go back to my father's home and live as a widow until his next son, Shelah, was old enough to get married. Again, the tradition was for a widow to marry the brother of her deceased husband.

But Judah didn't really plan for his younger, third son to marry me. He thought I was the reason his sons were dying. Me! The Bible says that both of his sons—my husbands—did things to anger God. That wasn't at all my fault. I was stuck in my father's house waiting on a promise that Judah never intended to make good.

What was I to do? Not much was expected from women other than giving birth to male heirs. I had had two husbands already—and I had no children. I could have stayed at Daddy's house, taken care of everyone else, and lived okay. But that just wasn't my destiny. And I felt it. I knew deep down that Judah was not going to give Shelah to me. And I knew deep down there was more in life for me. I wanted my more.

Have you heard the knocking at your heart's door? The tap that reminds you to keep looking? To keep seeking? Have you heard the hollow echo, reminding you that there is just more to life than this? My friend, I think your destiny is calling, beckoning for you to keep going and to find the reason you are alive. Your destiny cries out for you to keep looking and to keep pushing. This, where you find yourself right now, is not all you've been created for. There is more—something more fulfilling, more meaningful, more significant—for you to do.

Designer of Destiny: I desire more. I know you're calling me to something more and something else.

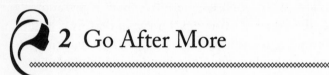

2 Go After More

When we trust in him, we're free to say whatever needs to be said, bold to go wherever we need to go.

Ephesians 3:12 (MSG)

A woman's worth was based on bearing an heir, and I was wrongly shunted aside because both my husbands had died before I could conceive. Judah, my father-in-law, promised to obey our people's cultural tradition, which meant he would have his third son marry me; but Judah had no intention of letting us get married. He lied and left me to grow old in my father's house.

I took action. I had to right this wrong. I had to do something drastic. I am not proud of the way I conceived an heir, but I did it. And later, I got Judah to confess that I was in the right and he was in the wrong (Genesis 38:26). I made Judah confess what *he had done and lied about.*

I went after what I thought was mine. But most importantly, I gave birth to not one, but two heirs. They are listed in the lineage of Jesus.

Birthing my twins, Perez and Zerah, was not an easy feat. I had to step out and go after my "more." I didn't know exactly what would happen or how things would turn out. I endured some shameful times. Many thought I was crazy. Others called me unthinkable names. But I had to go with what I felt inside of me. I knew there was more to this life. Although I didn't always know what my "more" looked like, I knew that I was called to more than a life of a lonely, mistreated widow. I had something greater to contribute to the world.

In my way, I impacted history. I pushed to give the world the one who would have another child who would have another and another—until we got Jesus, the Savior. My bold actions set my destiny into motion.

Times have changed, and living as a woman mistreated by men doesn't have to be a death sentence. But if you want to meet destiny and live out your life's purpose, you're going to have to boldly and courageously answer the door when you hear the knock. When you know that what you are doing right now or the way you're living right now is not enough, you're going to have to get up and get moving. Forget what others may say; forget what you've been told. You're going to have to go after your "more," your destiny.

All Powerful One: Give me strength and courage to go after my destiny.

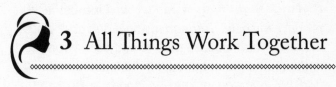

3 All Things Work Together

We know that all things work together for good for those who love God, who are called according to his purpose.

Romans 8:28 (NRSV)

This verse epitomizes what happened to me. Everything that happened to me was not good—in isolation. But somehow, when you add all of those ugly and terribly unfortunate things together, something beautiful developed.

Losing one husband is not good. Then being given in marriage to another who refuses to give you an heir at a time when that is a woman's claim to fame—that's really not good. And then waiting on my dear old father-in-law to give me the son he promised—but knowing that it really wasn't going to happen—is definitely not good.

But if you've read my story (in Genesis 38), you re-

alize that someway God made my not-so-good into good. Even when I did the unthinkable—I posed as a prostitute to trick Judah into sleeping with me— God took that situation and weaved it together to produce my heirs. Through my bold and audacious actions, Judah realized that he had been wrong to withhold his son from me. He had lied to me and had no intention of making good on his promise. But, even in the midst of that craziness, things worked out for my good. All of the pain, shame, and disappointment I went through worked together to produce something very good.

Going through life, you may not be able to see how a deceitful relationship, a job loss, a bankruptcy—whatever ugly you may face right now—is going to work for good. But as a believer in God, trust in the Word of God. And the Word says that things work together, things are woven in a God-type of way, to produce good.

What do you do while you wait for that good? Keep trusting. Keep pursuing your purpose. Keep looking for it, asking: "Why am I here? Why did God create me?" And your very reason may lie just beyond that last heart break. Maybe what you will learn from that ugly situation will set you on the course of your destiny.

Much like an old quilt, God can take the discarded

pieces of fabric and the leftovers from something else and join together a unique patch-worked design that shows the world not only beauty but purpose. It can be all good—if you press on and keep the faith.

Lifter of My Head: I will not be discouraged by life's situations and broken promises from others. I know that you are a promise keeper and can weave together something beautiful from the broken pieces of my life. I anxiously wait to see good come from my life's ups and downs as you bring me closer to my destiny.

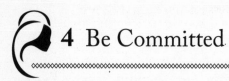

4 Be Committed

Whatever you do, work at it with all your heart, as working for the Lord, not for human masters, since you know that you will receive an inheritance from the Lord as a reward. It is the Lord Christ you are serving.

Colossians 3:23-24 (NIV)

I know my actions to grasp my destiny were not popular. I was pushed aside to wither up and die—even though my father-in-law, Judah, had promised me another husband so I could produce an heir. (Read my story in Genesis 38.) For a while, I sat around in my daddy's house and waited. But deep down, I knew it wasn't going to happen. Judah didn't want me to marry his son; Judah thought I had somehow caused the death of his other sons. That was not true, and I knew their deaths were not my fault. But even more importantly, I knew I had been called to

*more than a life in my father's home without a fu-
ture or a legacy. I was born to bear fruit, and I went
after my destiny with all I had.*

*I was committed to getting Judah to see how he
had wronged me. I devised a plan, and I had to be
courageous to see it through. I wasn't sure how
it would work out, but I needed to work that plan
to the best of my ability. I needed to be brave and
I needed to be bold. This was about more than just
me. It was about my destiny and my legacy. I had to
be committed and work hard.*

When you know you've been called to more
and truly want to follow your destiny, you've
got to be committed. You have to do like I
did and push toward your destiny, no matter what. It
can get hard. It can be unpopular. But if this is what you
know you need to do, then do it. And do it with all you
have inside of you.

If you are going to get to your destiny, you are going
to have to invest in yourself. And investing in yourself
takes commitment. It's not always going to be easy, and
it's not always going to be popular. But when you know
you've been called to a place, you've got to give it all you
have to get there. If you know you were meant to bear
fruit—through your work and how it reaches people—
you've got to push and press.

Investing in what it takes to get to your destiny is worth your sacrifice and your hard work. Your personal investment requires commitment. You have to hang in there with Destiny, even when it isn't looking good for you. Popular or unpopular, appreciated or not, encouraged or not, understood or not, hold on to Destiny and don't let go. Take a vow and declare your commitment to Destiny's unfolding in your life.

And always remember that you are working for God, putting in all of your effort to become who and what God has called you to be and to do. When you see God as your ultimate boss, you can give a little more because you desire to do what God calls you to do—because that's got to be something outstanding and life-altering. Renew your commitment to working for God to obtain your destiny. It's well worth the hard work.

Omnipotent God: Grant me the strength to commit to working for you each day as I strive to reach my destiny. I know you have called me to do more and to live a fulfilled and purposeful life.

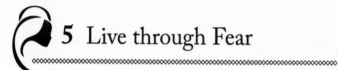

5 Live through Fear

For the Spirit God gave us does not make us timid, but gives us power, love and self-discipline.

2 Timothy 1:7 (NIV)

When Judah faked me out and did not give me his youngest son, I found myself basically between a rock and a hard place. Judah had no intention of giving me another one of his sons. He sent me to my father's house to wither and die (see Genesis 38).

I was lonely and afraid and scared and in a bad way. I was stuck in my father's house waiting. And waiting. Waiting on Judah to do what he promised—although I knew he wouldn't come through. I eventually had to make a decision. Would I sit and wait on what was not going to happen, or would I find a way to walk in my destiny and grasp what

*was mine? It was a frightening situation, but stay-
ing the same was even more frightening.*

*I had to figure out a way to get Judah to admit
that he was wrong and give me what was owed
to me—it was my destiny. Things could have gone
wrong, and for a while it seemed like they were. But
I faced my fear and did what I had to do. I couldn't
stay a slave to fear any longer. I figured I would either die a widow, mad and bitter because of Judah,
or die trying to meet my destiny. I had to give it a try.*

Fear can be paralyzing, and it can keep you from
your destiny. Fear can keep you in the same position, afraid to move although you know life won't
change if you don't take hold of the reigns and make
some changes. If you want to meet up with your destiny,
you're going to have to make a decision about fear. Yes,
moving into new territory, stepping out on faith, doing
what you haven't done before will seem scary and make
you fearful at times. But if God has truly called you to a
task toward your destiny, God has to make a way.

When you have faith in God, fear takes a back seat.
Fear cannot lead the way. Instead, the Spirit of God's
power, love, and self-discipline should take front seat
and lead us to victory. Notice I didn't say that the fear
wouldn't be there; it just cannot drive the ship. Sometimes, you are going to have to move even though you

are fearful. You're going to have to pray, seek wisdom, and jump.

You have to decide if you are going to live with the threat of failure or live forever as a slave to fear. When God calls you into Destiny, you may not know if you're doing it right or not; but keep going forward anyway. Yes, you may fail—this time, maybe even next time, or the time after that. Get up. Try again. Keep going. Get over your fear of failure because that is worse than actually failing.

Provider and Promise-Keeper: Thank you for replacing my spirit of fear with the Spirit of power, love, and discipline. I will move and live according to your Spirit this day.

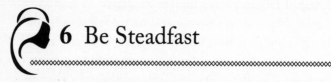

6 Be Steadfast

Therefore, my beloved, be steadfast, immovable, always excelling in the work of the Lord, because you know that in the Lord your labor is not in vain.

1 Corinthians 15:58 (NRSV)

When my daughter, Tamar, came back home after the deaths of her first and second husband, she was pretty dejected. She felt hopeless—as if her life was over. But I reminded her that she should not let her circumstances stop her. If she thought she was created with a specific destiny in mind, then she should do whatever it took to get to it.

Yes, what Judah did to Tamar was wrong. But Tamar couldn't let this situation keep her from her destiny. I had real conversations with my beloved daughter. I asked her if this was how she wanted her life to end. I asked her if she wanted to give her pow-

*er over to a man who lied to her and deceived her,
or if she wanted to find the strength to keep going
and to grasp hold of her destiny. I encouraged my
daughter to keep pushing, keep praying, and keep
seeking for an opportunity to grasp Destiny.*

*It was not easy; the system of the day was set
up to keep her down. But she eventually found the
courage and strength and fortitude to get what she
needed to reach her destiny.*

Your current circumstances don't determine the rest of your life. It is important to know what your destiny looks like so you can be steadfast in going after it. Sometimes, when we are not sure what will truly fulfill us, we can settle for imitations and short cuts. Or, we can become discouraged with our current set of circumstances and foolishly believe that things will never change.

A true Destiny follower will need to pack a great deal of fortitude and perseverance on this journey. It's not for the weary, and it is not a sprint. You will need to persevere. Pray. Look. Seek. Pay attention to the yearning inside of you and go after it, no matter how bleak conditions appear. It's worth the fight. It's worth the journey. It is worth the perseverance.

When the road gets rough and you get tired, remember that this journey is not in vain. There is a meaning to it. There is fulfillment in living your purpose and your destiny. Keep your eyes on the prize. Keep your feet to the fire and your hands to the plough. Your hard work and perseverance will pay off—even when it doesn't look like it.

My God and Friend: Keep me focused on my destiny as I run this race. When I am tempted to give up or give in, remind me to persevere so I may get the reward.

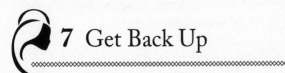 **7** Get Back Up

xxxxxxxxxxxxxxxxxxxxxxxxxxxxxxxxxxxxxxxxxxxxxxxxxxxxxxxxxxxxxxxxxxxxxxxxxxxxxx

[God is] right there with you. [God] won't let you down; [God]
won't leave you. Don't be intimidated. Don't worry.

Deuteronomy 31:8 (MSG)

My daughter-in-law, Tamar, was one resolute wom-
an. She was determined to meet her destiny, and she
did what she had to do to grasp it. I (Judah) didn't
help her at all. In fact, I did wrong by her. I foolishly
thought she was the reason both of my sons died;
and I didn't want to lose another son, so I lied to
her (Genesis 38). I told her to go back to her father's
house and wait for my third son to grow up. I had
no intention of letting my third son marry her. But
Tamar didn't let my deception stop her from reach-
ing her destiny.

When she realized that I wasn't going to make
good on my promise, she set out to trick me. She

*ended up unveiling my own deception and hypoc-
risy. That took a lot of courage and guts, but Tamar
wanted to reach her destiny. I know when she had
the twins and the connection to Jesus' lineage, she
felt like her risks were all worth it.*

The person who quits or gives up after a setback is not Destiny-bound. These people are afraid, so they pass up opportunities. They don't want to get knocked back down. I understand that getting knocked down hurts and causes bruises and fear. But you've got to take the risk if you want to meet Destiny. When you are down, tell yourself to get back up. Decide not to settle. I've had to fight to keep going. You will have to fight to keep going.

Maybe you always wanted to be a veterinarian, but flunked Biology 101. Maybe you've always wanted a catering business, but you ended up taking your first client to small claims court. There will always be challenges and setbacks, and no one is immune to a slip and fall on the journey to Destiny. Get back up and try again! Don't settle for the least out of life because you think you're not strong enough to get back up and try again.

Ever-present God: I know you have promised to be with me, and I know you are a promise keeper. Give me strength to get back up when I am knocked down.

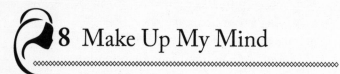

8 Make Up My Mind

Summing it all up, friends, I'd say you'll do best by filling your minds and meditating on things true, noble, reputable, authentic, compelling, gracious—the best, not the worst; the beautiful, not the ugly; things to praise, not things to curse. Put into practice what you learned from me, what you heard and saw and realized. Do that, and God, who makes everything work together, will work you into his most excellent harmonies.

Philippians 4:8-9 (MSG)

I had to get my mind set and determined before I could make my move toward my destiny. When I was first sent back to my father's house by my father-in-law, my mind told me I would not get married again and could forget about ever producing an heir. I had so many negative thoughts running through my mind: I was angry at both husbands for being foolish and selfish. I was angry at Judah for making a false promise to me. And I was even angry at God for taking my husbands and allowing Judah to go on lying to me.

But in order for me to reach my destiny, I had to break free of those chains on my mind. The negativity wasn't getting me anywhere. Those negative thoughts only made me depressed and hopeless. But I thank God that I was able to change the channels in my mind. Instead of replaying all of the horrible things that had happened to me, I began believing again. I believed that I was created with a purpose, and I believed that I would be able to reach my destiny. My road to meeting up with Destiny really began when I changed my mind and started focusing my energy toward God's promises, instead of man's.

When looking to follow your purpose and reach your destiny, examine your mind and see if you have taken off any chains that might block you. Everything you have been through, whether heavenly or horrific, will serve a meaningful purpose in your life if you allow it to. The pain you have been through, the losses, the humiliation, and the betrayal are all stepping stones to a higher place in Destiny, if you are willing to take the chain off your brain.

Have you considered whether your mind is open and

free to explore the path that God has set for you? Or, are you going through life like your brain is chained, locking up creativity and ideas? Free your mind and you will create a mental and spiritual environment for greatness.

Examine yourself. Know what you believe. Know your ideas. Know what you stand for, and know what has shaped your beliefs and ideas. Get rid of negative thoughts—and people who help you think negatively. Stuff has happened to you that is unfair, but it doesn't have to stop you from pursuing your purpose and reaching your destiny. In fact, some of the negativity can be turned into stepping stones to propel you toward the place you should be.

Make up your mind that you are not going to be held back anymore. Take the chain off your brain and develop new hope and new thoughts. You cannot change what has happened to you in life, but it certainly doesn't have to restrict your life. Make up your mind today to move forward and be determined.

Mind-Regulating God: Take the chains of negativity off of my mind. Free my mind so that I may focus on productive thoughts that give me hope and purpose.

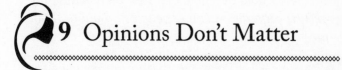

9 Opinions Don't Matter

*The LORD makes firm the steps of the one who delights in him;
though he may stumble, he will not fall, for the LORD upholds him
with his hand.*

Psalm 37:23-24 (NIV)

*May I remind you that I don't have a clean record or
a sweet story about how I reached my destiny? But,
may I also remind you that Jesus was born through
my son's lineage? That's right, even with my crooked
past, I contributed to society in a big way. I still met
my destiny even though I was the talk of the town. I
learned during that time that people's opinions just
don't matter.*

*Everyone didn't know my story; everyone didn't
know how Judah and his sons deceived me. Only
God knew my full story. So when I heard people
whispering and wondering how I got pregnant*

without a husband or how I tricked my father-in-law, I kept walking and I learned to hold my head up high. I knew what I was doing, and I knew that my children would be great. I was set on reaching my destiny, regardless of other people's thoughts about me.

People who knew me during my younger years would not have chosen me to do what God has positioned me to do. Back in West Virginia, when I was working in a chemical plant and preaching when opportunities arose, I would not have been the number one pick to have a thirty-thousand-member international ministry. Most would have expected me to take over my father's custodial services business.

At every turn of my life, people speculated how I would end up, where I would be, or what I would do. And most of the time they were wrong. That's why opinions don't matter. Often, God chooses the least likely to get the promotion, grant, spouse, or prize.

Right now, somebody doesn't think you're qualified to do what you're doing or have what you have. They don't think you're smart enough, wealthy enough, sexy enough, skinny enough, or friendly enough—a mother who doesn't think you're good enough to marry her son; a socialite who thinks you have no business moving into her gated community or doorman building; a business mogul who thinks your entrepreneurial ideas belong in the toilet. Their opinion is nothing more than their interpretation of you. They do not understand or know you, and they are not privy to your destiny.

Allow yourself to listen to those voices and you'll spend a lifetime defending yourself and your actions. If they get wind of your Destiny vision, they are likely to say, "You, of all people, will never make it happen." That's their opinion. Ignore them. Your future depends solely on what God has created you to do.

Creator and Purpose-Giver: Thank you for the path you have chosen for me to walk. Remind me that you and only you have created me for my destiny. I rely upon you to reach it, not the opinions of others.

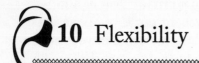# 10 Flexibility

Even when the way goes through Death Valley, I'm not afraid when you walk at my side. Your trusty shepherd's crook makes me feel secure.

Psalm 23:4 (MSG)

I learned to try several different routes to get what I needed. I didn't let failure stop me; I just looked at it as an opportunity to try something else. Once I realized that my life wasn't turning out quite like I had planned, I had to shift my thinking and my attitude. Losing one husband was bad enough. But then I lost another husband. And then my father-in-law decided to stop me from marrying his next son, which was not right according to the law. I could have given up on ever getting an heir. But instead of sulking and rehearsing how badly my life turned out, I thought of another plan.

I thought of another way to get to my destiny. I didn't let one roadblock stop me from finding another path. I felt driven to produce an heir—and when I did, one of my twins became a vital part of the connection to Christ, our Savior. Imagine if I would have let a detour keep me from trying to reach my destiny.

When you are on your road to Destiny, you develop a flexible mindset. While you are focused on making it and following your path, you are also very aware that when one roadblock is put up, you can adjust your navigation system and go another route. There's more than one way to get to your destiny. When you've made up your mind to follow the path, don't get bent out of shape when you have to take a detour—it may be a new route, but it will get you to your destination.

It's hard to continue moving in faith toward Destiny when life doesn't go the way that you'd planned. One of the hardest things for people to do is to trust and believe God when in transition. But if we will remain flexible and seek God for a new path, we just might find that Destiny awaits us—in a new place and in a new space. Bend to see the possibilities that are ahead of you.

Provider and Protector: Remind me to remain flexible throughout the changes of life. I trust you as life twists and turns. I know you will guide me in the way toward my destiny.

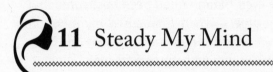 **11** Steady My Mind

People with their minds set on you, you keep completely whole,
Steady on their feet, because they keep at it and don't quit. Depend
on GOD and keep at it because in the LORD GOD you have a sure
thing.

Isaiah 26:3-4 (MSG)

Even while I was forced to raise two boys alone, I knew I was following my destiny. Somehow, I got the strength to continue to raise my sons and to keep moving forward despite the circumstances around their birth. Throughout the journey, I learned to keep my mind focused on God and the promises of God. Although my circumstances didn't always look promising, I knew God was a promise keeper. I had heard about the things God had planned for God's people, including me. I knew I was a part of that covenant agreement, and I believed.

So when my mind would wonder and I would begin to doubt, I tried to remind myself of all that God had promised. I reminded myself that I was not alone even though I had been mistreated and judged by others. When I refocused my mind on God, I was renewed. I knew I had a destiny and I was able to run this race with my mind focused.

We all hear voices that can have an impact on our Destiny decisions. We have to decide which voices we will heed. The voices that you pay attention to are the ones that will manifest in your life. If you've turned your heart and your head toward Destiny, you must train your mind to hear positive, affirming voices that offer wisdom.

Rehearse what God has told you. Rehearse God's Word concerning you and your destiny. These are the voices you need to keep on repeating. Play them back in your mind as often as possible. It's how you get to your destiny.

Prince of Peace: I will repeat your promises daily so that I can tune out the critical voices. I will keep my mind centered on you and your promises.

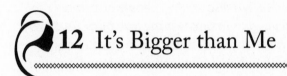 **12** It's Bigger than Me

xxxxxxxxxxxxxxxxxxxxxxxxxxxxxxxxxxxxxxxxxxxxxxxxxxxxxxxxxxxxxxx

Do nothing out of selfish ambition or vain conceit. Rather, in humility value others above yourselves, not looking to your own interests but each of you to the interests of the others.

Philippians 2:3-4 (NIV)

When I first started thinking of a plan to leave my daddy's house and gain my rightful stake in Judah's family, my main goal was to get back at Judah, my father-in-law, for what he had done to me (Tamar). But as I prayed and prayed, I realized that finding my purpose and meeting my destiny couldn't be about getting back at Judah. It couldn't even be all about what I wanted for my life. It had to be bigger than that.

I realized that in order to have true success and true meaning in this life, it had to be centered on God's plan and God's will. I had to ask God many

*times why I was placed here on Earth and what I
was supposed to do. I needed to know what I was
really supposed to leave as my legacy—not only to
bless myself, but also to bless people after me.*

*When I began to discover my true purpose, I was
able to move forward. I was able to go after my destiny—even when roadblocks threatened to stop
me. When I knew this was bigger than me, I had the
strength and determination to fight for my destiny.*

D estiny is bitter when pursued just to prove
something. If you envision Destiny as proof of
something to someone, stop right here. Back
up and figure out who you are, who you want to be, and
why. You need a strong identity to pursue Destiny.

The secret is that your destiny has to be bigger than
you. For even if by a miracle your self-serving dream
comes to fruition, it's not going to be what you hoped if
it's only for you, or your ego. A desire to serve humanity,
help your family, or improve yourself is stronger than
your ego. Your ego motivates you to succeed because of
how your success will impress others, but that is empty
and unfulfilling.

Stay faithful to Destiny's demands. Destiny is bigger
than you and your dream must be also.

God of Mercy: Forgive me for pursuing destiny for selfish reasons; help me to release anything that is not pleasing to you so I may run this race without the weights and burdens of getting back at others. I desire to live the life you have purposed for me.

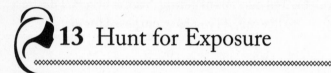

13 Hunt for Exposure

Whoever goes hunting for what is right and kind finds life itself—glorious life!

Proverbs 21:21 (MSG)

When I made the courageous decision to leave my father's home and go after what Judah promised me, I also learned the value of exposure. I had been pretty sheltered most of my life. But going after Judah brought me to new places; not all of these places were places I wanted to stay or revisit, but I learned more about the world and how people navigated through it.

On the journey to get what was rightfully mine, I met new people with new ideas and new cultures. It was definitely a journey—and I learned more about others, as well as more about myself and what I wanted out of life. I'm thankful for my journey and all it produced.

Destiny constantly gives us opportunities for exposure to the new, different, greater. And those who are exposed benefit from all they take in. When you experience new cultures and new people, you learn to see the world from different perspectives. You learn to think of ideas from different perspectives. You don't throw away your experiences and culture. (How could you?) Instead, you add to your outlook with the help of others. It's a great symphony, coming together to create something one instrument alone could not produce.

A powerful, pivotal catalyst for life change is exposure to new facts, ideas, cultures, languages, and information. When you go hunting—seeking adventures throughout this life—you will find life itself, a "glorious life!"

Exposure teaches you that there is more than one way of doing things and that there are not necessarily right or wrong ways, just different. Exposure teaches you that many life decisions are about choosing differently, rather than some universal imperative that requires people to live a certain way. Embrace the exposure you gain from pursuing Destiny's path.

Guiding Light: Lead me on this journey as I'm exposed to new people, places, and things. Keep me on the path you have called me to as I embrace exposure.

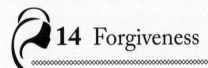14 Forgiveness

But when you are praying, first forgive anyone you are holding a grudge against, so that your Father in heaven will forgive your sins, too.

Mark 11:25 (NLT)

I could have stayed mad at my father-in-law—and even at my dead husbands— but I knew I needed to change my focus and my perspective to be successful on my journey. When I was mad and upset and unforgiving, I felt heavy. I was burdened. But when I finally was able to let go and tell myself that I was more than a victim, I was able to think of a way to get on with my life and have purpose.

Forgiveness was not just about my husbands and their father; forgiveness was about freeing myself up to run life's race. I couldn't be weighted down with negativity and bitterness. I had things to do. I had Destiny to meet. I needed to be free to soar.

Charles Swindoll has been attributed with this observation: "Life is 10 percent what happens to me and 90 percent how I respond to it." The perspective you take on life's flow and transitions makes the critical difference. The decision to proceed in life, no matter what, is why some thrive in transition while others wither.

The decision to forgive or let go is also critical to your survival. From a biblical viewpoint, it is how we continuously receive God's forgiveness—by forgiving others. It's part of a cycle. But forgiveness also frees us from the weight of bitterness and negativity. Letting go frees you to be more productive and energetic—giving you tools you need to get to your destiny.

Gracious and Forgiving God: Thank you for the cycle of forgiveness. I release my bitterness so that I can soar and meet my destiny.

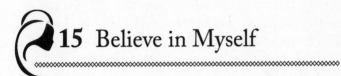

15 Believe in Myself

God, the LORD, created the heavens and stretched them out. He created the earth and everything in it. He gives breath to everyone, life to everyone who walks the earth.

Isaiah 42:5 (NLT)

I didn't have an easy life; but I believed in myself. I believed I had what it took to live a different life. I rose and gained the courage to do what I needed to do to get to my destiny. I knew God had created me for more, and I found the strength and courage to go after it. I believed.

It takes courage to produce what God is drawing out of you. It means you must rise to a higher level, an unknown place that offers no guarantees about what will happen when you get there. In a culture that worships success yet asks, "Who are *you* to think you can be successful?" it takes courage to believe you can contribute something.

Who are you? You are not rich, and neither is your daddy. You're not famous or powerful. The ads you see in the media say you are not good-looking. How dare you believe God has a fulfilling destiny for you? Who are you to dream of success? No matter what success looks like for your life, my destiny is to confirm that the door to Destiny is open to anyone with the courage to knock—just like Tamar.

Destiny Maker: I believe you have a destiny planned for me. I believe I can reach the place you've called me to. I will walk forth in faith.

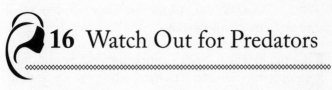16 Watch Out for Predators

xxxxxxxxxxxxxxxxxxxxxxxxxxxxxxxxxxxxxxxxxxxxxxxxxxxxxxxxxxxxxxxxxxxxxxxxxxxx

"Surely the righteous still are rewarded; surely there is a God who judges the earth."

Psalm 58:11(NIV)

You intended to harm me, but God intended it all for good. He brought me to this position so I could save the lives of many people.
Genesis 50:20 (NLT)

My two husbands and their father were selfish and really only looked out for themselves—no matter what they told me. Although they were supposed to protect me and take care of me, they didn't. They did the exact opposite. They really were like predators, lurking upon me to suck the life out of me and then leaving me to wither and die. They were not interested in helping me reach my destiny and become all God had created me to be.

But those men didn't get the last word in my story. God had another plan. I was still able to follow my destiny, despite what those men did. They couldn't block what God had just for me. They actually set me up to reach my destiny.

It's important to watch out for evildoers and fake people in your life. Knowing who you are dealing with will help you plan. But ultimately, learn to trust in God and depend on God. When God has a plan for you, humans can't stop it. In fact, their very works can be turned around for your good and for God's purpose. It's amazing how God works.

When looking at the horror show that can sometimes be life, be aware of predators—those who want to suck life out of you and keep you from your destiny. Much like the classic vampire of the modern horror genre, a predator is often smart, cunning, and physically attractive. When he comes after you, he'll usually be smooth, even charming. He studies his prey, chooses carefully, and lures you in before the strike.

Classic vampires take longer to recognize because they are engaging, charismatic, and they may engross you in stimulating conversation. They are dangerous because, ultimately, they suck out your life force. They don't care about your hopes, dreams, or destiny. They're predators who want to drain you dry.

Stick close to God to avoid predators; and when you do encounter them, trust God to turn their dangerous schemes into your good.

Sustainer and Protector: I thank you for being able to turn evil into good. I rejoice, knowing that no person can stop me from reaching my destiny. I press on knowing that you are working things out for me.

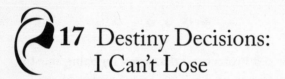

17 Destiny Decisions: I Can't Lose

×××

God knew what he was doing from the very beginning. He decided from the outset to shape the lives of those who love him along the same lines as the life of his Son. So, what do you think? With God on our side like this, how can we lose? If God didn't hesitate to put everything on the line for us, embracing our condition and exposing himself to the worst by sending his own Son, is there anything else he wouldn't gladly and freely do for us?

Romans 8:29, 31-32 (MSG)

I would have never made my move if I waited to be 100 percent sure. I knew I wanted to pursue my destiny and not waste my time away in my dad's house waiting on my father-in-law to do what he said. I had several plans, and I knew several things could go wrong. In fact, some did. But I had determined that I was going to keep going no matter *what. I just felt deep down that God would help to make everything right—if I did my part. So instead of being afraid of making the wrong move or of being embarrassed (or even stoned in my case), I used that energy to gain courage and strength to make my move. I figured with God on my side I couldn't lose—no matter how things turned out.*

With Destiny, you've got to take a few chances. If you've prayed and prayed and gathered the information needed, you're going to have to jump and go for what you feel called to do. Sometimes people wait and wait until they are absolutely sure of everything before they can make a move. Sometimes we move timidly, as though there is only one precise step we can make; and if we don't make the right one, all of our hopes and dreams will collapse. That's simply not true. Always strive to make your choices based on sound information, and then move forward. There will be times when you decide based on a hunch or a feeling. Pray about it and follow that choice. You will find that even when your decision was not the best, God can still use the situation to bless and propel you toward Destiny.

When God is for you, there's not much that can keep you away from your destiny. When you truly believe that, you can put aside fear and pick up courage. God has an amazing way of bringing you to your destiny when you put your best foot forward, too. Be less fearful and more faith-filled so you can keep moving. If you believe that you can't lose, you can walk boldly and fiercely into your destiny.

My Redeemer and Refuge: I have decided to continue to walk in my destiny. I refuse to let fear paralyze me and keep me from moving. I will walk in courage and faith and trust that you will make my path clear. I know I can't lose when I am in your will.

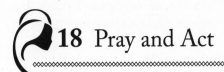

18 Pray and Act

Dear friends, do you think you'll get anywhere in this if you learn all the right words but never do anything? Does merely talking about faith indicate that a person really has it? Faith and works, works and faith, fit together hand in glove.

James 2:14-15, 18 (MSG)

When I sat in my daddy's house fuming over what my father-in-law had done to me, I prayed and prayed for God to make things right. It just wasn't fair that my father-in-law would tell me to wait for his next son when he had no plans of delivering on his promise. I was waiting and waiting for things to change. Then, one day, it hit me: I needed to do something!

Prayer is definitely needed in all situations, but I also had to move and put things into motion. I prayed without ceasing and then I had to get up and do something. I was fearful, but I kept praying and I kept moving. I wanted to meet my destiny and walk in it, so I kept that in mind every time I was tempted to stop and run back to my dad's home. I kept my mind focused on new levels, new living, and my destiny. It was worth it.

There are some things you have to do to release what God has prepared for your life. It is not going to happen in spite of you; it will only happen because of you. Saying, "Whatever happens in my life is all right with me," is not choosing Destiny. Now is the time for you to make the decisions that will empower you to rise. God will give you glimpses of Destiny, but you may not know how to get there.

When I was a boy, God began giving me peeks at my destiny, but I had no idea at the time how I would get there. I now can see how, time and again, I was elevated to a larger arena. Each time a place became confining, I was able to rise to another level. Each new level was bigger, so I could grow. As I arrived in those larger spaces, I had to learn new skills. In each new environment, I was able to order and steady my steps, gain new confidence, learn from new exposure, and absorb new knowledge.

If you are serious about walking in your destiny and living the life you are created for, I implore you to keep going no matter what. Keep moving and keep looking, knowing that God may be calling you to another level. Don't fear learning something new, walking in new arenas, and getting new exposure and knowledge.

All-Knowing God: I am open to all you have for me. I want to learn new things and walk in new arenas. I know you will provide me with all I need as I step out and explore.

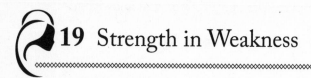19 Strength in Weakness

><<<<<<<<<<<<<<<<<<<<<<<<<<<<<<<<<<<<<<<<<<<<<<<<<<<<<<<<<<<<<<<<<<<<<<<<<<

My grace is enough; it's all you need. My strength comes into its own in your weakness.

Once I heard that, I was glad to let it happen. I quit focusing on the handicap and began appreciating the gift. It was a case of Christ's strength moving in on my weakness. Now I take limitations in stride, and with good cheer, these limitations that cut me down to size—abuse, accidents, opposition, bad breaks. I just let Christ take over! And so the weaker I get, the stronger I become.

2 Corinthians 12:9-10 (MSG)

Mine is not a pretty story, and I don't try to glorify what I did; but I did have to learn to focus on God for strength and not on myself or others. As I continued my journey toward my destiny, I had to stop beating myself up and repeating negative things others said about me.

When it was tough to keep going on to fulfill

my destiny, I had to remember that God was my strength. I had to stop focusing on how I had gotten on this path and start focusing on what God had called me to do. When I felt like giving up or like I didn't have what it took to live a fulfilling life, I looked to God—and I found strength.

In the end, I realized that fulfilling my destiny really wasn't about me; it was about God. That took the pressure off and made me know I didn't have to be perfect. I didn't have to get it right every time. God was with me, and that is really what mattered.

God's opinion is the only one that matters. Listen to what God tells you. Then watch what you say to yourself. Don't tear yourself down. Don't beat yourself up. You cannot arrive at Destiny if you tell yourself you're not good enough, not smart enough, unqualified, unattractive. Don't work against God by tearing yourself down.

Reaching Destiny requires that you monitor how you talk to yourself and know that, even in the areas of your weakness, God can provide strength. In fact, God can become a stronger presence in your life in those areas. So don't consider them weaknesses; consider them God-strengthening areas.

Next to the voice of God, your own voice is the most important one you will hear. You are with you all the time, so guard how you talk to yourself. You can avoid negative people, but you can never get away from yourself. You can't escape yourself. If you're tearing yourself down, you must change your thoughts from negative to positive and from destructive to uplifting. Build yourself up by speaking self-empowering words. Ward off "iffy" talk—like "I wonder . . . ." and "What if . . . ." It is nothing more than negative speculation.

Guard your mind against speculation about your destiny. You can't have what you are striving for in your hand until you have it in your head. Get it into your head—not your feelings—that you can and will achieve your goals. Whatever you want, get it in your head by changing what you think and say. God is your strength.

My Strong Tower: I know you are my strength in my weakness. Help me to rehearse your might and power instead of repeating my shortcomings. I know I can do all things through your strength.

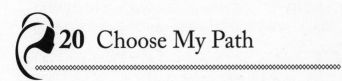

20 Choose My Path

Show me the right path, O LORD; point out the road for me to follow. Lead me by your truth and teach me, for you are the God who saves me. All day long I put my hope in you.

Psalm 25:4-5 (NLT)

I was tempted many times to stay put and let life happen to me. I sometimes fooled myself, and I pretended that I was living a happy life and that I had been given what I was promised. It's how I got through some days. But in the end, I just had to launch out. I had to give it a try. I had to go after my destiny—in whatever way it came about.

I couldn't stay the same and sit in my comfort zone. Quite frankly, it just wasn't that comfortable knowing I wanted more and that there was more for me to find. So I took a leap of faith and went after what I thought was my destiny. My actions may

*have been unconventional, but I did end up follow-
ing the path I know I was called to follow. It was
scary. It was hard. It was not always fun. But I did it.
I left the comfort zone and walked toward my destiny. I wasn't going to be able to sit still without trying.*

Take on the challenge of seeing who you can become. Ignore the deceptive lure of the comfort
zone. If Destiny is calling, you can never be
satisfied with sameness and mediocrity. And if you're
afraid to leave the comfort zone, think about this: if you
leave the comfort zone to pursue Destiny and it doesn't
work out for you, you can always go back to the comfort zone. Those same people you left will still be there
when you get back.

You get to choose where you will dwell: comfort zone
or creative zone. If you are brave enough to ignore the
distractions, you will feel as if you have arrived home
when you get to the creative zone that is your destiny.
Your ideas will be embraced and celebrated. You will
know you are on the right path.

**Living God: Lead me and direct me into the creative
zone. I desire to leave behind the comfortable so I can
press toward my destiny.**

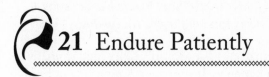21 Endure Patiently

Then the way you live will always honor and please the Lord, and your lives will produce every kind of good fruit. All the while, you will grow as you learn to know God better and better.

We also pray that you will be strengthened with all his glorious power so you will have all the endurance and patience you need. May you be filled with joy.

Colossians 1:10-11 (NLT)

When I set out on the journey, I had no idea how long it would take to truly reach my destiny. Sometimes I worried that I'd never get to do all of the things I knew I had inside of me and was destined to do. Sometimes I thought I'd be stuck in my father's home or stuck in the web of lies Judah created (Genesis 38). But because I was certain that I wanted to live out my destiny, I kept going. I decided to be in this pursuit of Destiny for the long haul.

I thank God for the strength to keep moving and endure all I had to go through to reach my destiny. It was worth every long night and rough day.

Going after your destiny takes determination and patience. It may be a long road, and only the strong will truly stick with it. As people watch you make sacrifices to invest in yourself, they will want to invest in your dream, too. When you are busily engaged in personal investment, God sends people from out of nowhere to support you, encourage you, and invest in your dream. You may not even be aware that they're watching you, but they will show up and amaze you.

Investing in yourself requires determination—the kind that knows Destiny is worth never giving up. The determination you have to invest in yourself says that even if no one else believes in you, you do. Even if no one else can see what's inside of you, you do. Be determined to invest in you despite delays, setbacks, sidetracks, and turnarounds.

God of My Weary Years: I thank you for being patient

with me as I journey toward my destiny. I need your
   strength to endure this race with patience.

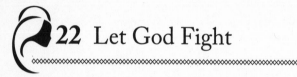

22 Let God Fight

"This is the word of the LORD to Zerubbabel: 'Not by might nor by power, but by my Spirit,' says the LORD Almighty."

Zechariah 4:6 (NIV)

If it had been up to me, I would have told Judah what I wanted and what I needed—so I could get on with my destiny. But that's not what God would have. That was not the culture of my time. I knew that not every battle could be fought out right and in my timing. I learned that for some things, I had to wait on God and on God's timing.

God's timing is critical if we're going to get to our destiny. And we've got to learn to rely on it. Sometimes in our do-it-yourself culture, it can be difficult to distinguish when to go forth and when to stand still. But as you seek to follow your destiny, it will be important to be in tune to God's leading. It is critical to know when to move and when to stand still, when to fight and when to sit back and watch God work things out in a miraculous way.

If you're a make-it-happen person, you may be trying to do it all—doing battle every day to make your dreams come true. Your hindrance? Trying to build your dream without the Dream Maker. Getting to Destiny involves so much more than what you can do. Know this: when God works in the midst of your goals, you will reach them. You definitely have a role to play, but so does God.

Distinguishing God's responsibility from your own is hard. Praying regularly for guidance can remind you that you are not a lone ranger. God's power and Spirit is greater than yours. You can't always see what is around the corner or know how one move will spark another move in a domino effect, but God can and does. By relying on God's Spirit to know when to move and how to move, you yield to your greater Power. You acknowledge that God has a plan for you and God has a timing to bring things to bear.

When you feel a nudge and a pull to sit back for a minute and rely on Someone other than yourself, relax. Think about all of the ways God has come through for you in the past. Read about Bible personalities and people you know personally. Look for their testimonies. Use all of these examples—including yours in past situations—to continue to build your faith and to know that the right time and right circumstance is coming. Your job is to be ready when it comes.

Don't grow weary fighting for yourself. Not all battles need to be fought by you with your own weapons. Wait and watch things unfold to bring you closer to your destiny so you can impact more people.

Warrior God: Remind me that you can fight my battles.

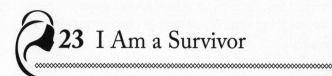

23 I Am a Survivor

No, despite all these things, overwhelming victory is ours through Christ, who loved us.

Romans 8:37 (NLT)

Although my story isn't pretty and it took lots of guts, tears, and prayers, I can declare loud and clear: I am a survivor. I came through the long, hurtful road of lies and deception, gossip, and hurtful words to grab hold of my God-given destiny. Even though my route was unconventional and scandalous, I persevered. I picked myself up. I kept moving forward. I kept my goals in my front view and refused to look back.

And through it all, I was able to give birth—even though Judah denied me his promise and my right. I was able to give birth to not one, but two boys. I was able to be the link between Judah and Jesus.

My destiny produced an heir to the eternal throne. I am a part of the holy lineage. I played my part; and through it all, I survived. I birthed my destiny and lived a fulfilled life—one that carries on after me. I survived. I thrived. My destiny left behind an eternal legacy.

In the midst of this journey, sometimes you have to take a look at how far you have come and celebrate. Many didn't think you'd make it this far—you may not have even believed—but you did. You have a cloud of witnesses, like Tamar, to look to and to gain strength from. Her story wasn't easy, but she survived. She lived to fulfill her destiny. You, too, are a survivor. You've come through many trials and tribulations to stand today. So rejoice. Find strength in all God has allowed you to overcome.

Survivor, rejoice! You've overcome a great deal, and you have what it takes to live fully.

All-Sufficient God: I praise you because you have kept me on this journey. I know I can survive and thrive because of you.

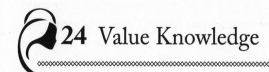

24 Value Knowledge

Wise men and women are always learning, always listening for fresh insights.

Proverbs 18:15 (MSG)

My story doesn't end with me getting Judah to admit that he had wronged me. In fact, that is really just the beginning.

I went on to take care of my twins so they could impact the future. I couldn't possibly take care of these two mighty men without learning all I could. I became a student and I learned constantly—how to help them and how to help myself. Life opened up when I opened my eyes and looked for new ideas and fresh insights.

My fight with Judah took a lot out of me, but my quest for knowledge renewed me and refocused me to complete my Destiny journey.

Knowledge is power, and you really can't have enough knowledge. When you chase down knowledge and wisdom, you keep growing. When you think you've learned enough or don't need any more information, you become stale and stagnant.

I've become increasingly concerned over a societal trend that can be best described as a dumbing-down of ideas. The acquisition of knowledge seems to have little value or meaning. We dumb down information to a 140-character tweet on *Twitter* or a brief Facebook post or a seconds-long YouTube video.

The knowledge you need for Destiny won't come in a tweet or any social media post. You won't see it on Instagram. You're going to have dig deeper to find it. The true Destiny seeker will have an insatiable quest for knowledge.

Destiny Giver: Provide me with a quest for knowledge that never ends. Help me to realize I will always need good information to continue my journey toward Destiny.

Tamar's Destiny Steps

Find a mantra to recite when you feel like your circumstances will not change.

Think of a person who got back up after a knock-down. Use that person's story to help you keep going when you are down.

Remain flexible on the path to your destiny.

Rahab's Story

Joshua 2:1-21 (NLT)

Then Joshua secretly sent out two spies from the Israelite camp at Acacia Grove. He instructed them, "Scout out the land on the other side of the Jordan River, especially around Jericho." So the two men set out and came to the house of a prostitute named Rahab and stayed there that night.

But someone told the king of Jericho, "Some Israelites have come here tonight to spy out the land." So the king of Jericho sent orders to Rahab: "Bring out the men who have come into your house, for they have come here to spy out the whole land."

Rahab had hidden the two men, but she replied, "Yes, the men were here earlier, but I didn't know where they were from. They left the town at dusk, as the gates were about to close. I don't know where they went. If you hurry, you can probably catch up with them." (Actually, she had taken them up to the roof and hidden them beneath bundles of flax she had laid out.) So the king's men went looking for the spies along the road leading to the shallow crossings of the Jordan River. And as soon as the king's men had left, the gate of Jericho was shut.

Before the spies went to sleep that night, Rahab went up on the roof to talk with them. "I know the LORD has given you this land," she told them. "We are all afraid of you. Everyone in the land is living in terror. For we have heard how the LORD made a dry path for you through the Red Sea when you left Egypt. And we know what you did to Sihon and Og, the two Amorite kings east of the Jordan River, whose people you completely destroyed. No wonder our hearts have melted in fear! No one has the courage to fight after hearing such things. For the LORD your God is the supreme God of the heavens above and the earth below.

"Now swear to me by the LORD that you will be kind to me and my family since I have helped you. Give me some guarantee that when Jericho is conquered, you will let me live, along with my father and mother, my brothers and sisters, and all their families."

"We offer our own lives as a guarantee for your safety," the men agreed. "If you don't betray us, we will keep our promise and be kind to you when the LORD gives us the land."

Then, since Rahab's house was built into the town wall, she let them down by a rope through the window. "Escape to the hill country," she told them. "Hide there for three days from the men searching for you. Then, when they have returned, you can go on your way."

Before they left, the men told her, "We will be bound by the oath we have taken only if you follow these instructions. When we come into the land, you must leave this scarlet rope hanging from the window through which you let us down. And all your family members—your father, mother, brothers, and all your relatives—must be here inside the house. If they go out into the street and are killed, it will not be our fault. But if anyone lays a hand on people inside this house, we will accept the responsibility for their death. If you betray us, however, we are not bound by this oath in any way."

"I accept your terms," she replied. And she sent them on their way, leaving the scarlet rope hanging from the window.

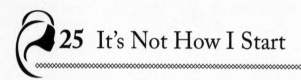

25 It's Not How I Start

By faith the prostitute Rahab, because she welcomed the spies, was not killed with those who were disobedient.

Hebrews 11:31 (NIV)

I'm a witness that where you start out doesn't have to determine where you end up. As you can tell from my story, I was a prostitute. It's what I did, and it's recorded all over the Bible. Every time you see my name, you see my beginning address: prostitute, harlot, etc. But my beginning is not my end. If you read my story carefully (see Joshua 2), you will see that not only was I destined to bear a child who would be in the lineage of Jesus, I also saved my family.

By faith, I listened to those men of Israel and did exactly what I promised them—I hid and protected them. In return, they did exactly what they promised *me. They did not destroy my family. I, Rahab, the harlot, saved my family from destruction because I had faith. I had heard about Israel and all their God was doing for them.*

Just because I had a bad reputation didn't mean I couldn't listen out and observe and act when called upon. Faith made me do that. I forgot what I did in the past and pushed forward, in faith, to do something new, something courageous, something that helped not only myself, but others.

Some think they can't amount to anything because of where they were born. Your destiny can take you to places much further than your beginnings. Whether you were homeless, abandoned, abused, mistreated in the beginning, you don't have to remain where you started.

Some people can get stuck on their past. They may not come from a good family; they may not have had the best opportunities growing up; they didn't come from the right side of the tracks. Your past does not have to determine your future. Instead of focusing on your past and what you didn't have, focus on having the courage to follow what you know is right inside; focus on believing that God will deliver on all promises.

It's not helpful to say why you can't do something, to blame your past. Things can be different, with faith and courage and action. Step out of your issues and into your destiny. Distinguish your true self from the circumstances surrounding your past.

Gracious God: Thank you for using me in spite of my past. Thank you for giving me a destiny. Help me to keep moving forward, looking toward my destiny and not focusing on my past.

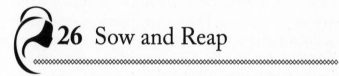

26 Sow and Reap

But the one who plants in response to God, letting God's Spirit do the growth work in him, harvests a crop of real life, eternal life.

Galatians 6:8 (MSG)

> I did a pretty risky thing. I put my life—and my family's life—at risk by hiding the spies from Israel (see Joshua 2). But this was a calculated risk. I knew I was being called to sow a little faith and do a little good. I felt inside of me that helping the spies was the right thing to do and that it would lead me to my destiny and others to theirs. I asked those spies to remember me and my family when Israel took over the land. If they were being led by God, they would succeed.

I n order to live your destiny, you're going to have to figure out when to sow and when to reap; when to plant a seed and when to pick it up. Walking in your destiny can be tricky and risky. You have to know when to plant and when to reap. You have to know when you need to do something to get something else.

On your route to Destiny, you have to decide when and where to invest. Every engagement you're invited to doesn't always require your "yes." Other times, you need to know that the exposure and experience you'll get for participating is worth the donation of your time and gift. You have to learn to balance and know when to give and when to take. Your gifts are worth something, and you have to set that price.

As I say in *Destiny*, "Be generous, until your generosity comes at the cost of your destiny." Remember, Destiny always pays its bills and gives returns.

Being intentional and discerning can help you decide which offers to accept and what to pursue. Your risks can pay off with major dividends.

Holy One: Show me when to move and when to stay put. Teach me to discern between when it is time to sow and when it may be time to reap.

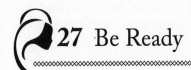# 27 Be Ready

Meanwhile, Joshua said to the two spies, "Keep your promise. Go to the prostitute's house and bring her out, along with all her family." The men who had been spies went in and brought out Rahab, her father, mother, brothers, and all the other relatives who were with her. They moved her whole family to a safe place near the camp of Israel.

Joshua 6:22-23 (NLT)

My occupation didn't stop me from being ready to seize an opportunity to save my family and step into my destiny. I somehow knew that it made sense to pay attention, to always seek knowledge, and, quite frankly, to be ready when opportunity came knocking. My mindset paid off for me and my family. You can read my full story in Joshua 2 and Joshua 6. Even though I was considered an enemy to the Israelites, I worked to help them. By helping them at the right time, I saved my family.

You may wonder how I knew that I could trust these Israelite spies. I had observed a lot in my day. I had heard about the Israelites and their God. I didn't limit myself to just finding out about the day-to-day gossip in Jericho, my home. I expanded my knowledge by listening and observing what people were talking about. So when it came time to make my move, I had enough information to know that these spies were real and their God was mighty. I had enough to know all that God had done and would do. I took my knowledge and applied it to the situation; I asked those spies to make sure my family and I were safe when they invaded Jericho. Because I knew what I knew, I was able to save my family.

It pays to have knowledge and to use what you know to get what you need. Knowledge beyond your current parameters can be your entre into your future. Many people limit themselves because they refuse to learn or look for information outside of their familiar territories. They are limited. And when opportunity comes, they are ill-prepared. When you are determined to live your destiny, you stay ready. You know that broadening your knowledge level will expose you to new people and things—some of which you will need to use in your destiny.

Consider reading new blogs, new authors, new genres. Perhaps you don't like hockey or hip-hop music, but a little exposure to them won't hurt. It could make the difference in connecting you to your destiny. Go places you've never gone. Open your eyes and see what is around you in this world. Therefore, when God opens the door, you won't need to get ready; you will be ready. The reward can be great.

All-Knowing, Living God: I vow to open my eyes and grasp knowledge and new opportunities. I want to be ready to meet my destiny.

28 Trust God

Trust in the LORD and do good. Then you will live safely in the land and prosper.
Take delight in the LORD, and he will give you your heart's desires.

Psalm 37:3-4 (NLT)

I know you want to know how I knew I could trust the spies that came to my house one day in Jericho. The story of how I saved those spies is a part of my story and a part of my destiny. I am recorded throughout history as the one who saved the spies and therefore saved my family. My answer is that I trusted God. I may not have had my life totally together, but I had heard about the God of Israel and all that God had done for the people.

I heard miraculous stories; I heard stories of protection and provision. I believed every one of those stories, and I put my trust in that very same God. I thought: I want to be on the side of Israel's God. So I started thinking about those stories and just meditating on what kind of God would care so much about people and protect them and deliver them. I wanted to serve that God.

So I knew that those spies were telling the truth. I knew that they would protect me and my family if I would just hide them for the night. My destiny was beckoning, and I walked toward it. I trusted first and then acted. And my decision paid off for me and my family—and all of creation.

I n my book *Instinct*, I talk about the inherent aptitude or capacity to use your emergent, God-given gifts effectively at the appointed time and place. Instinct is the urging inside of you that tells you to make your move now, to reach out now, to hold back until later, or to never give up. Instinct must merge with purpose to give you life that fulfills your destiny. All gifts must be given a place of expression in order to unfold Destiny.

We are most effective when we yield to the wooing allure of Destiny! Every gifted person needs a place to engage the gifts that are rooted inside. No matter how gifted you are, you need a place of expression. Your instinctive gifts are the metal inside you. Your destiny is the magnet that draws you to that predestined arena where you use your gifts.

And when you are looking for your destiny, lean and depend on God. In fact, Scripture tells us to delight ourselves in God—revel in who God is and all God has already done. When we find ourselves delighting in God, Scripture says God will then give us our desires. If it is your desire to meet Destiny, start by trusting and delighting in God.

Heavenly God: I delight in who you are and all you have done for me and for others. I want to spend this day reveling in your awesomeness.

29 Gifted Me

A gift opens the way and ushers the giver into the presence of the great.

Proverbs 18:16 (NIV)

I may be written about in the annals of the Bible and throughout history as a prostitute; but I had much more to share with the world and my gifts helped to bring about my destiny. I learned some lessons early on about gifts. I had many come to me who just wanted me for a moment. But I never let my identity get wrapped up in what people wanted from me. I was more than the title they gave me.

Because I knew who I truly was and I had observed the goodness of the God of Israel, I was ready when the spies approached me to help them. They didn't show up like all the other people in my life. They came seeking my help. They came looking for an-

other gift I had. They understood who I really was—a believer in God. My true gifting made room for me. My true gifting gave me the opportunity to help Israel take over Jericho. I played a part in their destiny. I played an essential role in the lives of those spies and the entire kingdom of God.

K now that God has a plan for you to use your real gift. So don't get caught up in what others call you or what others think about you. Be true to your God. Be true to yourself—and you will be able to discern when it is time to use your gifts to fulfill your destiny. People will try to use you for what they can get out of you. If you're a very gifted person, people will seek you out. They will call upon you constantly to share your gifts for one purpose or another.

Today's Bible passage says your gifts will make room for you and propel you to higher places. It is beautiful to witness your gifts open doors for you to run a corporation, play basketball, write, paint, remodel, practice medicine, teach, cook, nurture, or whatever you are gifted to do. When you are really good at your gift and work to hone your skills, people will constantly request your services. Being sought after can make you feel loved and admired. It can make you feel worthy. But don't confuse the gift with you.

I've learned not to let how others define me affect

me. People are attracted to gifts; it's natural. But you need to protect yourself and your gifts from what others have to say. Your gift is from God and should be presented back to God as a thank you. How you use your gift shows how you thank God. Be you. Be authentic. Separate yourself from the gift others see—so you don't get caught up in your own hype. Don't delay your destiny by getting caught up in the gifting. Be true to your God. Be true to yourself.

God of Truth: Keep me truly authentic. Help me to see my gifts and remember that gifts come from you and should be used for you. Remind me that I am not my gifts. I am not what people see. I vow to remain true to you and true to my calling.

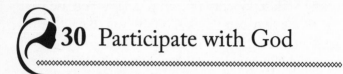

30 Participate with God

So you see that a person is shown to be righteous through faith-ful actions and not through faith alone. In the same way, wasn't Rahab the prostitute shown to be righteous when she received the messengers as her guests and then sent them on by another road? As the lifeless body is dead, so faith without actions is dead.

James 2:24-26 (CEB)

My actions show that faith and works combined will help you get to your destiny. I believed in the God of Israel. I believed all of those amazing stories I heard passed down. I knew that God was with the people and wanted to bring about the best for them. And because I had faith and believed, I was able to act.

I didn't just pray for a miracle to happen; I partici-pated in a miracle happening. By believing in the God of Israel, I helped the spies—even though I was risking my life. I hid the spies; that was my work. I trusted that they would protect me when it came

*time to take over Jericho; that was my faith. Togeth-
er, I participated with God to help the spies get the
information they needed to take over Jericho and I
saved my family.*

Some think faith is a one-way street. They believe
in God and wait on God to do the work. They
think belief is the only thing they need. Others
have the warrior spirit. They forcefully go in and take
whatever they need, regardless of what time it is and
what season it may be. They don't pay much attention
to internal clocks. And while all warrior all the time can
be detrimental, the opposite can be, too.

The polar opposite to the warrior spirit—the wimpy
spirit—makes me crazy. That person does nothing but
sit still and procrastinate, waiting for God. They say,
"Well, I'll just pray about it." They use waiting on God
as an excuse for their own lack of engagement. "If God
means for me to have it, I'll have it," they mutter.

Destiny will not appear on your doorstep and intro-
duce herself. Although there is a spiritual dynamic to
Destiny, it is not solely spiritual. *You* have to be engaged
in the process. God definitely plays a role, but so must
you. Again, that divine-human partnership is tough to
figure out. But as the saying goes, "Work as if Destiny
depends totally on you, and pray as if it all depends on
God."

Active and Dynamic God: I readily participate with you in bringing about my destiny. I know some things can only be done by you; and some things can only be done when I take a step.

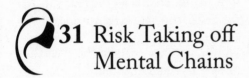

31 Risk Taking off Mental Chains

<<<<<<<<<<<<<<<<<<<<<<<<<<<<<<<<<<<<<<<<<<<<<<<<<<<<<<<<<<<<<<<<<<<<<<<<<<<<<<<

So be strong and courageous, all you who put your hope in the LORD!

Psalm 31:24 (NLT)

If I had stayed in the same place and never taken a risk, I would not have met my destiny. I had to forgo the normal and the comfort of the same, day-in and day-out existence. I had to stretch myself beyond what I knew and even how I was raised. I had to be courageous.

When I was approached by the spies from Israel (Joshua 2), I thought about not helping them, but then I really thought about my choices. I could keep doing what I was doing and wait for something to change, or I could take a risk and do something different. I could help the spies, whom I knew were sent by God. And, even though I knew of the great deeds of God, I still had to think for a minute about my risky deed.

I'm thankful to God that I didn't let the fear of the unknown and the fear of the new keep me back.

D o you have the courage to take the chain off your brain, even when the person who put those chains there is someone you love and who loves you? In spite of that love, they accidentally incarcerated your creativity. But prison is prison, whether intended or not.

Think about how you were reared—whether by a mother who worked as a waitress and could barely pay the rent in the trailer park where you lived, or whether you grew up like the Huxtable family of the popular *Cosby Show* television comedy of the 1980s and 90s. All of what you have experienced plays a role in Destiny, even the situations and people you must choose to leave behind in order to arrive there.

Merciful and Almighty God: I need your strength to be brave and courageous. I desire to take off the chains of normalcy and stretch beyond my comfort zone.

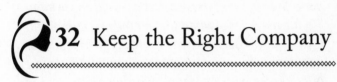

32 Keep the Right Company

~~~~~~

Now then, since I have dealt kindly with you, swear to me by the LORD that you in turn will deal kindly with my family. Give me a sign of good faith that you will spare my father and mother, my brothers and sisters, and all who belong to them, and deliver our lives from death."

Joshua 2:12-13 (NRSV)

He who walks with the wise grows wise, but a companion of fools suffers harm.

Proverbs 13:20 (NIV)

I had been living in Jericho for a while. I had heard about the God of Israel and the things God was doing for Israel. I wanted to be in that company. I wanted to be on the right side. I wanted to be on the side of the God of Israel. So when the opportunity presented itself, I made a decision. I was going to follow the people who followed God.

I decided to help the spies from Israel. I hid them in my house; and when the men of Jericho came looking for the spies, I told the men that the spies were gone. In fact, I sent those men on a wild chase looking for the spies—when I knew they were really in my house. My decision was strategic. I was ready for new company and new associations. I had to start hanging out with the people who were going in the same direction I wanted to go. That decision saved my life and my family's life and helped me reach my destiny. I'm glad I kept the right company.

If you want better out of life, sometimes you've got to do better—and that can mean changing your associations. In *Destiny*, I share a story about a working, but poor man who grew weary of living with limited resources. When he looked around at his friends, he realized that he had one friend who had accrued wealth. This rich friend wasn't smarter or more gifted than his other friends; but somehow, he had amassed wealth. So the poor man asked his rich friend to tell him his secret. The wealthy man said: "Keep the right company."

The poor man took the advice to heart. He observed that all his other friends hated hard work and had no desire to improve themselves. So the poor man started making new friends by attending conventions and seminars to connect with successful people. He eventually made a list with two columns; one column included people who would improve his life by association, and the other column listed those who could drag the man down.

He then decided to spend as much time as possible with those who could improve his life and less time with those who could bring him down. Within three years, the man was a millionaire.

The company we keep influences us in more ways than we can realize. Surround yourself with Destiny seekers and limit your time with those who are drifting through life. You want to purposefully live around those who are living on purpose.

God, My Companion: Give me the audacity to align myself with wise, Destiny seekers and the courage to limit my times with drifters.

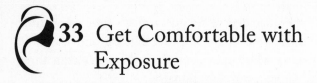

33 Get Comfortable with Exposure

Now the gates of Jericho were securely barred because of the Israelites. No one went out and no one came in . . . . But Joshua spared Rahab the prostitute, with her family and all who belonged to her, because she hid the men Joshua had sent as spies to Jericho— and she lives among the Israelites to this day.

Joshua 6:1, 25 (NIV)

When I decided to step out on faith and side with the Israelites, I was exposed to an entirely different culture—and it wasn't always easy. I made a deal with the Israelite spies (Joshua 2) because I believed the miraculous things their God had done for them. And those spies delivered on their promise to me. When they took over my city of Jericho, they spared me and my family and all of our belongings.

I was sad to see the others taken down. But soon I

realized that I had stepped out of my comfort zone and chose to be exposed to something different. This act saved my family and me. I needed to be grateful for the opportunity and the willingness to live with new people. If I hadn't been exposed to the wonderful works of the God of Israel, I would have been destroyed, too. I had to get comfortable with my new life and new exposure and my path to my destiny.

When you choose exposure and have the courage to see another side, it could take a little getting used to. You may feel like you don't fit anywhere: new situations are so unfamiliar, and you've outgrown the old. You might worry about whether the new people you're meeting will accept you. You may have so many unfamiliar and unsettling feelings from this exposure that you will begin to think, "Maybe I made a mistake." You'll question yourself, "Maybe I don't belong in this world." And maybe you don't, but exposure is what teaches you whether you do or not.

You may be experiencing anxiety from unfamiliar territory, or you may decide a thing is just not for you. Part of the challenge to gaining more exposure is pushing past the feelings of discomfort as you acclimate to your new environment. Get comfortable. Become familiar with new ways. Invest in an appropriate wardrobe so you won't be self-conscious. It's all a part of your exposure.

The Great I Am: I desire to move into a new place and be exposed to new people and ideas. Grant me comfort in accepting the new things and the new world to which you allow me to be exposed.

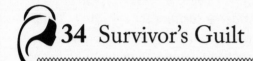

34 Survivor's Guilt

"Besides, who would patch old clothing with new cloth? For the new patch would shrink and rip away from the old cloth, leaving an even bigger tear than before. And no one puts new wine into old wineskins. For the old skins would burst from the pressure, spilling the wine and ruining the skins. New wine is stored in new wineskins so that both are preserved."

Matthew 9:16-17 (NLT)

Some may wonder how I was able to turn on my people of Jericho and help the spies of Israel. I already mentioned that I had observed the workings of the God of Israel, and I believed. I knew God was a miracle worker and able to do anything. I also wanted to be in the company of believers—others who had witnessed the power of God and had put their trust in God, too.

So when the day came when Jericho was de-

stroyed and my family was spared, I was not happy that my people had been destroyed; but I also didn't feel guilty. I had listened to the same stories others had heard. I chose to believe and I chose to be courageous and make a sacrifice for my family. I had put in the hard work and trusted in God. Now, I was reaping the benefits.

It's sometimes hard to grasp when you're chasing after your destiny that not everyone will want to make the same sacrifices as you. If you are going to be successful and fulfilled, you're going to have to accept this harsh reality and do your best regardless of what others say or do.

Survivor's guilt can affect those who successfully escape a life of poverty or dysfunction. Guilty for having worked their way out of those circumstances, they are tempted to bring along others they knew before who did none of the hard work, who are only interested in the perks of success, or who cannot leave inappropriate behavior behind. The successful are often accused of forgetting where they came from. They feel guilty and try to maintain friendships with people who are not going anywhere.

Destiny does not require you to continue to surround yourself with people from a life you worked hard to escape. You don't have to act like you're better than them, but it is not wise to pretend you all are still the same. When you've put in the work, you shouldn't feel guilty enjoying the benefits.

Your new mindset needs a new environment to thrive in, not the old. Jesus taught that you wouldn't use new material to patch old clothes or put new wine in old containers. The same remains true today; the new you will need a new environment, reflective of your goals.

Almighty One: I am grateful for my destiny and the new places you are taking me. I thank you for being by my side every step of the way. With great anticipation and hope, I boldly walk into my new environment.

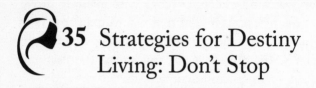

35 Strategies for Destiny Living: Don't Stop

×××

Stay with GOD! Take heart. Don't quit. I'll say it again: Stay with GOD.

Psalm 27:14 (MSG)

When I shared with some friends that I wanted to do better, live a different life, find fulfillment and my purpose, I had people cheering me on. I had people who wanted to join me in figuring out a plan and living differently. But let me tell you, when things got serious, when we had to make a move, when we had to make a decision, not everyone was up for the task.

I kept going. I kept my plan in sight. I did what I had to do to go after my destiny—even when that meant leaving some people behind. It's what I was determined to do. I'm sorry they didn't come along for the entire journey, but I'm glad I was able to take my family to a new and better place.

When you start out on the path to chase your destiny, you may have many on that same road. Everyone gets excited about going after something better, but not everyone will be there for the long haul.

The journey to Destiny can operate like a horror movie script. You may have started out with a group of friends, fellow students, co-workers, or business partners who were determined to fulfill their purpose and live in Destiny. Along the way, some couldn't fend off attacks. And now you, too, have to watch out for the person you once dreamed dreams with because they may turn and attack you.

Horror movie survivors keep moving in the midst of terror. They don't stop to ask "why" questions. Feelings of betrayal and hurt are natural responses when people or events wreak havoc on your Destiny journey; but bind your wounds and keep it moving. Glance back and cry for a bit; but you don't have a lot of time for whys. God owes you no explanation for allowing painful circumstances. God has only promised to be with us and provide comfort during those times.

Rest in the assurance that God is with you. If you ask the person responsible for your trauma, he or she probably couldn't explain it. Just like the flesh-eating zombie or vampire pursues prey because that is their nature, the undead in your life derail your destiny because that's all they know to do.

My Great Lord: I thank you for the courage to keep moving no matter what. I know my destiny awaits me, and I've answered the calling.

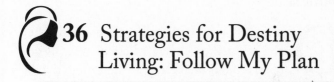

36 Strategies for Destiny Living: Follow My Plan

The LORD will fulfill [The Lord's] purpose for me; your steadfast love, O LORD, endures forever. Do not forsake the work of your hands.

Psalm 138:8 (ESV)

As I journeyed in this life, I developed a vision. I saw my life changing. I decided I no longer wanted to be the prostitute, the one everyone sought for their own pleasure. I saw my life having a bigger purpose. I saw my family living a different life. I slowly began to develop a plan—one that meant leaving Jericho and finding more fulfillment.

I waited for the right time and I waited for the right opportunity—then I made my move. I had to change things sometimes, but my plan was always before me. I knew, somehow and some way, I could live differently. I was determined to follow my plan and create a destiny for myself and my family. I trusted that the vision God had given me would be fulfilled.

Destiny followers need to have a plan and they need to stick to it. Regardless of what is going on around them, they are determined to be the protagonist in their own life script. If you seek your Creator when developing a strategy, God will let you know it's the right one for your life.

When you have a strategy to fulfill your life's purpose, you may have to make some adjustments as circumstances change, but stick with the plan. A plan has room for flexibility, but it doesn't deviate from its purpose. The compass is always pointed forward—that is part of the strategy.

Keep going. Get back up if you fall down. Follow your strategy to fulfill your destiny.

Gracious and Omniscient God: I praise you for the vision you have given me. You are awesome and all-knowing. I trust you completely and will follow your plan.

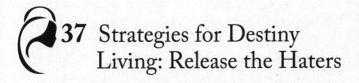

37 Strategies for Destiny Living: Release the Haters

If then there is any encouragement in Christ, any consolation from love, any sharing in the Spirit, any compassion and sympathy, make my joy complete: be of the same mind, having the same love, being in full accord and of one mind.

Philippians 2:1-2 (NRSV)

Once I put in place my plan to bring about my God-given vision of living a purposeful life, I realized that some people around me were just not happy about my new plans. While I was still walking toward my destiny and setting things into motion, those who used to be my friends were saying negative things and creating blockages in my plan. I'm not completely sure if they intended to do this or if they just didn't know how to handle a Destiny seeker.

It saddened me to realize that some people were

just not ready to live complete and fulfilled lives. They were not ready to make a change, and they didn't get the "new" me. They were comfortable living as dead people—without a vision, without dreams, without a plan to follow their purpose.

One of my family members told me that if I truly wanted to meet my destiny, I'd have to lessen my contact with these types of people. They were bringing me down, and I needed to save my energy to keep going. I needed to be filled with courage, not doubt. I needed to be around life, not death. I had to make the choice to leave those people behind.

In my metaphor of horror movies, I'd like to remind you that Destiny seekers do not court the undead. The undead are those people we often love, but who are just not living. They are comfortable being dead even though their heart is beating. They are comfortable not dreaming even though they still have breath in their bodies. I called them the undead. They are not of the same mind as Destiny seekers.

It is dangerous to still live with and spend too much time with these types of people. The undead enjoy infecting other people and sucking life out of them. You don't have the luxury of hanging around people who have no purpose and have given up on bettering themselves. Lessen your time around them—and if need be and if possible, release these haters from your life. You'll be in a better position and better mindset to reach your destiny if you do.

Jehovah-Jireh: I acknowledge that you have always provided everything I've needed in life. Even when people try to bring me down, I know you can lift me up.

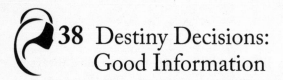

38 Destiny Decisions: Good Information

xxxxxxxxxxxxxxxxxxxxxxxxxxxxxxxxxxxxxxxxxxxxxxxxxxxxxxxxxxxxxxxxxxxxxx

For which of you, intending to build a tower, does not sit down first and count the cost, whether he has enough to finish it?

Luke 14:28 (NKJV)

Happy are those who find wisdom, and those who get understanding, for her income is better than silver, and her revenue better than gold.

Proverbs 3:13-14 (NRSV)

When the Israelite spies showed up at my house and asked me to hide them, I wasn't afraid to make my move toward my destiny. I had been waiting for my chance to align myself with the right side. I had done my research and I had collected enough data about the God of Israel. I had listened to the miraculous stories, I had observed other people from Israel, and

I had enough data to know that God was with Israel. I knew that God was delivering on some promises to Israel and I wanted in.

So when I had to choose whether to hide the spies or give them up to the officials of Jericho, I wasn't afraid to make my move. I reviewed my information and gained strength from all that I had heard and witnessed. I was making the right choice. I then asked the men of Israel to make sure they remembered me and my family—and they did. Because of the information I had, I felt confident in my decision. My research paid off and helped me put my faith into action.

Sometimes, it is not courage that we lack in order to make a decision; it's information. Good information can bolster our courage to make Destiny decisions. It's terrifying to make a decision in the darkness of ignorance. You *should* be scared to make decisions with no information. Good information can unfreeze the paralysis of your mind and enable you to make a Destiny decision. Before you build a house, common sense says to count the cost. You don't just start building a house without knowing how much time and money it will cost you. Whether you're quitting your job to return to school, changing careers, or changing your relationship status, get good information. Once solidly informed, make your Destiny decisions.

You can't make great decisions with erroneous information. I watched a television program one night about a judge who was about to rule on whether or not to extend a stay of execution for a man who was condemned to die by lethal injection. Everything was prepared for the execution. However, on the day before the scheduled execution, the condemned man's attorney presented new information to the judge. The information he provided changed the convicted man's life. With the new data the judge received, he spared the man's life. When you're about to make a Destiny decision, get all the accurate information you can. When you've got a good idea of what you're coming up against, you can muster the courage you need to keep going.

Almighty and Merciful God: I want to make informed decisions. I will collect information and pray so I can make Destiny decisions. Help me to discern the way to my destiny.

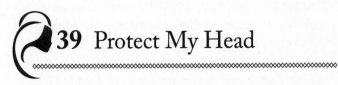

39 Protect My Head

From now on, brothers and sisters, if anything is excellent and if anything is admirable, focus your thoughts on these things: all that is true, all that is holy, all that is just, all that is pure, all that is lovely, and all that is worthy of praise.

Philippians 4:8 (CEB)

I'm known throughout the Bible for my courageous acts that saved my family, but the path toward my destiny was not always faith-filled. I had to learn to cast away the negative feelings and thoughts within my head to move forward and live the life I was called to live. When I hid those Israelite spies, I was not very popular. Some people knew about it and talked about me. When I heard what they said, brave ol' me got scared. I wondered if I had done the right thing. I wondered about the future of my family and whether the Israelites would hold up their *end of the bargain (Joshua 2).*

I could have driven myself crazy with "what ifs" and "I wonders." That is exactly when I learned that I needed to get my mind right and focus on the positive. I needed to focus on even more than the positive—I needed to focus on what God had done in the past for the Israelites and what I knew God would do for me. And even after my family's lives were spared, occasionally doubt and fear would peek into my life and make me wonder if I was on the right path. I had learned my lesson by then, and I quickly turned my mind toward all the things I had to praise God for.

When you've been through some tough stuff, you can recall it to get your mind right for the next leg of the journey. When I thought of God and all God had done for me, I could keep moving. I could dispel negative, fearful thoughts and push forward.

Look at any soldier, football player, or even biker who is seriously involved in their sport and you will find protective head gear. These warriors understand the importance of having the right head gear. And if you're serious about making decisions that put you in line with your destiny; you, too, will need some protective head gear.

Above all else, guard what goes on in your head. Protect that space between your ears with all you've got! A soldier about to go into battle, a police officer about to make a raid, a football player headed for the playing field will each protect his head with the proper gear. Protect your head so that your journey to Destiny is guided by knowledge rather than feelings. Protect your head to keep negativity out.

When people doubt your abilities, when you have an attack of low self-esteem, or when you experience a setback, don't fall into a dark place from which you cannot easily emerge. Preserve your positive thoughts. Keep your thoughts in a good place. Protect the positive person inside you who is telling you that you have what it takes. Watch your self-talk. Tell yourself you will make it—no matter what happens, no matter what anyone else thinks. Don't let other people's negativity stop you; and don't let your own negative thoughts hold you back. Think on the things that are true, holy, just, pure, and praiseworthy; these thoughts will cancel out the negative.

My Lord and Redeemer: Forgive me for not always protecting my mind from negative thoughts. Renew

my mind and help me think of your praiseworthy deeds throughout this day.

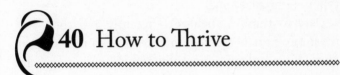

40 How to Thrive

Souls who follow their hearts thrive.

Proverbs 13:19 (MSG)

I knew that I wanted to go after my destiny and I'd have to follow my heart. I couldn't just stay in the same place and do the same thing. I had done that already, and I wasn't living. I wanted to thrive. I wanted to follow my heart's passion and live differently. It was in me, and I had to unleash all that God had placed inside of me.

I got up and moved on; even though it meant leaving some right where they were—in their own comfort.

Comfort zones don't have a favorite neighborhood. In the most prosperous neighborhoods, just as in ghettos, people are confined: they marry only a certain type, enroll children only in certain schools, drive certain cars, shop in particular stores, maintain accepted political affiliations, and join specific types of organizations.

Dare to think or behave differently and soon you must move on, becoming an outcast from the comfort zone. The people who live there fear the non-compliant among them, fear creativity because of its boundless abundance, and fear visions and imaginings that cannot be contained or controlled.

Destiny seekers live in the creative zone without limits or boundaries. Their energies are stirred by the creative process. Creative zoners thrive on new ideas and designs. They await new expressions of imagination to energize and enliven them. Like comfort zone dwellers, creative zoners come from every walk of life, socioeconomic group, race, gender, and educational level.

Holy and Loving Creator: I want to live. I want to thrive. I vow to release my comfort and pursue my destiny.

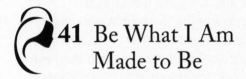

41 Be What I Am Made to Be

✕✕✕

In this way we are like the various parts of a human body. Each part gets its meaning from the body as a whole, not the other way around. The body we're talking about is Christ's body of chosen people. Each of us finds our meaning and function as a part of his body. But as a chopped-off finger or cut-off toe we wouldn't amount to much, would we? So since we find ourselves fashioned into all these excellently formed and marvelously functioning parts in Christ's body, let's just go ahead and be what we were made to be, without enviously or pridefully comparing ourselves with each other, or trying to be something we aren't.

Romans 12:4-6 (MSG)

I could have said that I was only a prostitute, a sinner lady with no hope of having a destiny. But instead of focusing on what others had, what I didn't have, or my past, I decided to use what I had to get *what I wanted.*

Now I'm not talking about using my body to get favors; that's not how I met my destiny. I used my experience and knowledge as a prostitute to talk to the spies and to talk to the Jericho officials. I realized I was comfortable around men—and many women of my time might not have been. I realized that I was in a position to help the spies and to save my family. I used this to get to my destiny. I may have wanted a different past, but that's not what I had. By focusing on what I did have, I was able to ensure a better future for my family and me.

Your experiences make you who you are. It's true. Don't run from them; use them to point you to the path you are destined for. If you come from the streets, you probably have a certain wisdom and understanding that can help you on your path toward Destiny. If you've had the opportunity to sit at the feet of great minds, use that experience to propel you to your destiny. No experience is wasted. No experience is meaningless if you're willing to take the lessons you've learned and apply them toward your destiny.

Don't curse your past or the dark times you've had to endure; use them as stepping stones to get to where you are destined to be.

Miracle-Working God: I marvel at your ability to use all of my experiences to direct me toward my destiny. I am in awe of your amazing power and wonderful plans. I praise you.

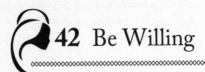# 42 Be Willing

I will praise you seven times a day because all your regulations are just. Those who love your instructions have great peace and do not stumble.

Psalm 119:164-165 (NLT)

When people look at me, I may seem like the least likely person to be written about several times in the Bible. I think it is because I was willing; I was ready to be obedient and follow God's directions. I was in a position to go, and I did just that: I moved.

I don't think it takes the most righteous person or the holiest person or the person from the right side of the tracks to reach Destiny. I think one of the most valuable characteristics is to be willing to open your mind and your heart to new possibilities and to follow God's instructions—wherever they may lead you.

It's important to remember that Destiny doesn't call out only to the most talented, the wealthiest, and the best educated. Destiny calls out to all of God's creatures. Our God, the same One who created the waters and the land, did not run out of creativity when you were born. You, too—no matter what others have said about you or what you've thought about yourself—have been created for a special purpose. You have a special gift or skill or way with words, people, money, clothes, wood, etc.; and it points to your destiny.

So instead of looking at all you don't have and wondering how in the world you will possibly pursue Destiny, make sure you have what Rahab had: a willing spirit. If you want your destiny, it will be revealed to you. Go after Destiny, willing to follow God's instructions with your heart, mind, and soul.

Great and Awesome Creator: I know you have fashioned a destiny just for me. I am ready and willing to walk on that path.

43 Explore All around Me

How much better to get wisdom than gold, to get insight rather than silver!

Proverbs 16:16 (NIV)

I kept learning and exploring all I could about the Israelites. Most people feared them because we had heard about the mighty acts of their God (parting the Red Sea, tripping up the mighty Egyptians, etc.). Not too many people wanted to cross the Israelites, but not too many people wanted to help them either. And that's where I saw my opportunity.

I set out to learn everything I needed to know about Israel and their God. I listened every time one of my customers talked about them. I sat quietly and listened to the people in the marketplace. I got all of the information that I possibly could get. I wasn't clear on how this would help me, but I knew it would point to my destiny.

If you're in search of your destiny, never stop learning, never stop exploring, never stop listening. What you learn today could be put into use tomorrow. Keep looking. Gain knowledge from unlikely sources.

Knowledge comes from all types of people and sources. Open your mind to opportunities to gain knowledge and take the time to engage with those who don't look like you or think like you or act like you. They can prove to be your life's greatest teachers. Let your quest for knowledge take you places you've never gone; so when God opens the door to Destiny that you've always wanted to enter, you'll be prepared.

All-Knowing and All-Powerful God: I desire to learn everything I need to know to meet my destiny. Open my eyes to take in all you will have me to know.

Rahab's Destiny Steps

Write a list of praiseworthy deeds you will keep your mind fixed on today.

Look for opportunities all around you to learn.

Make one bold step toward your destiny today.

Review your plan; determine to stick with it.

Ruth's Story

Ruth 1:3-18 (NLT)

Then Elimelech died, and Naomi was left with her two sons. The two sons married Moabite women. One married a woman named Orpah, and the other a woman named Ruth. But about ten years later, both Mahlon and Kilion died. This left Naomi alone, without her two sons or her husband.

Then Naomi heard in Moab that the LORD had blessed his people in Judah by giving them good crops again. So Naomi and her daughters-in-law got ready to leave Moab to return to her homeland. With her two daughters-in-law she set out from the place where she had been living, and they took the road that would lead them back to Judah.

But on the way, Naomi said to her two daughters-in-law, "Go back to your mothers' homes. And may the LORD reward you for your kindness to your husbands and to me. May the LORD bless you with the security of another marriage." Then she kissed them good-bye, and they all broke down and wept.

"No," they said. "We want to go with you to your people."

But Naomi replied, "Why should you go on with me? Can I still give birth to other sons who could grow up to be your husbands? No, my daughters, return to your parents' homes, for I am too old to marry again. And even if it were possible, and I were to get married tonight and bear sons, then what? Would you wait for them to grow up and refuse to marry someone else? No, of course not, my daughters! Things are far more bitter for me than for you, because the LORD himself has raised his fist against me."

And again they wept together, and Orpah kissed her mother-in-law good-bye. But Ruth clung tightly to Naomi. "Look," Naomi said to her, "your sister-in-law has gone back to her people and to her gods. You should do the same."

But Ruth replied, "Don't ask me to leave you and turn back. Wherever you go, I will go; wherever you live, I will live. Your people will be my people, and your God will be my God. Wherever you die, I will die, and there I will be buried. May the LORD punish me severely if I allow anything but death to separate us!" When Naomi saw that Ruth was determined to go with her, she said nothing more.

Ruth 4:13-17 (NLT)

So Boaz took Ruth into his home, and she became his wife. When he slept with her, the LORD enabled her to become pregnant, and she gave birth to a son. Then the women of the town said to Naomi, "Praise the LORD, who has now provided a redeemer for your family! May this child be famous in Israel. May he restore your youth and care for you in your old age. For he is the son of your daughter-in-law who loves you and has been better to you than seven sons!"

Naomi took the baby and cuddled him to her breast. And she cared for him as if he were her own. The neighbor women said, "Now at last Naomi has a son again!" And they named him Obed. He became the father of Jesse and the grandfather of David.

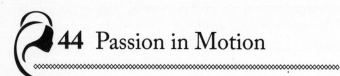

44 Passion in Motion

But Ruth said, "Don't force me to leave you; don't make me go home. Where you go, I go; and where you live, I'll live. Your people are my people, your God is my god; where you die, I'll die, and that's where I'll be buried, so help me GOD—not even death itself is going to come between us!"

Ruth 1:16-17 (MSG)

I'm Ruth, the one known for sticking by my mother-in-law's side. I said those words: "Where you go, I will go; where you live, I will live . . . ." I meant them. At the time I made that vow, I was in a new place in life. I was forced to make a fresh start. My husband—my mother-in-law's son, Mahlon—had died. My mother-in-law, who was already a widow, had no one else. Her other son, Kilion, had died, too.

I was young. I could have chosen to stay in my home country like my sister-in-law ultimately decided to do. I probably could have found someone else to marry and had some kids, but I just didn't think that was my destiny. I didn't feel passionately enough about staying in Moab. What I felt passionately about was helping my mother-in-law. She was older. She was not even from Moab. She didn't have a husband or her sons. She was all alone.

I wasn't quite able to put my finger on it, but somehow I knew that I was wired to care for people—and I was instinctively concerned about my mother-in-law. When she decided to return to her home in Bethlehem, I knew she needed a companion on that journey. How was this older woman going to take care of herself? What if she got attacked? What if she got sick? It was too long a journey for her to go it alone.

I cared. I wanted to take care of her. So I followed my passion. I felt strongly about taking care of my mother-in-law, and I vowed to go wherever she wanted to go. I was not going to treat her like an in-law. I was going to be her family. That was it. And, truthfully, that's all I knew. That's all I had to go on when I set out on that nebulous journey to Bethlehem.

Meeting your destiny often begins with a lone trip where we have no clue what lies ahead. If you know you are passionate about something (like writing, dancing, designing) or someone (like the elderly, youth, single mothers, fatherless boys), follow that passion. Perhaps you don't like the way immigrants are treated or you smile each time you see a child or you love helping people figure out finances—whatever your passion is, do it to the best of your ability. Do it to the fullest. Follow it wherever it leads you. Follow it passionately. You have no idea what awaits you on the other side. That passion will lead you to your destiny. When your instinct merges with passion, you get your destiny.

Awesome Almighty: Thank you for my passions. Help me to pursue them to the fullest so that I may meet up with my destiny. I look forward to seeing what lies ahead and living a fulfilled and meaningful life—for your glory.

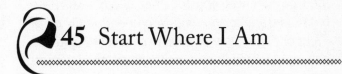

45 Start Where I Am

God can do anything, you know—far more than you could ever
imagine or guess or request in your wildest dreams!

Ephesians 3:20 (MSG)

I took that journey with my mother-in-law, Naomi. I
stayed by her side each step of the way; I felt like that
was what I was called to do. I think my destiny began
to be revealed when I followed that inner prompt-
ing that told me to do that—something that no one
else could do quite like I could. My destiny was found
in that little town of Bethlehem.

As I was following my passion of caring for my
mother-in-law, I was prompted to go out and find
food for us while we settled in Bethlehem (Ruth 2).
I went out in the harvest field to pick up leftover
grain. It was hard work, but I was called to care for
Naomi. I was called to take care of this woman even

though my husband was no longer living.

Who would have thought that while I was focusing on my personal conviction to take care of Naomi, God was weaving together another story—a bigger destiny for me and Naomi and really all of Creation? I just so happened to choose the field of a rich man named Boaz. He noticed me and my commitment to my passion, my mother-in-law. I ended up marrying Boaz. And the son we eventually produced would go on to be the grandfather of one of Israel's greatest—King David.

Look at God! By following my passion of taking care of my mother-in-law, I met my destiny. By following my passion, I played my part in the making of history and lived a life that was more fulfilling than I could have dreamed.

Follow your passion to see where your destiny lies. It just might blow your mind. Many wonder about their purpose and destiny. How do you get your instincts to guide you to the "why" of life? How do you know the "why" of your life? You were born for a distinct purpose in this life, even if you have yet to figure out that purpose.

Think of this life as a canvas. Every time you decide to draw on it, you are creating. You can use your time aimlessly doodling, or you can go after what you feel compelled to do. You can begin to draw a masterpiece, one stroke at a time, one color at a time. The entire picture won't come together at once, but you can start right where you are. And you can make the stroke you do today a good one, an intentional one. Today's stroke can be filled with passion, which will soon point you to your purpose and your destiny.

El Shaddai, Almighty God: I faithfully step forward today to fulfill my destiny. I will take one step forward fueled by my inner drive. I will give my all to develop the gift you have placed inside of me so that I can live the life you've called me to live.

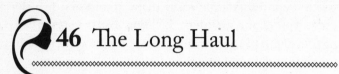

46 The Long Haul

And let us not be weary in well doing: for in due season we shall reap, if we faint not.

Galatians 6:9 (KJV)

My journey with my mother-in-law, Naomi, was not a quick, easy trip. When our husbands died, I made the decision to care for my mother-in-law. It's what I did. It's what I knew. It's what I felt was right. (Read more in Ruth 1-2.) We journeyed together from my home country of Moab all the way to Naomi's land of Bethlehem. It was not an easy journey. Naomi was mad and bitter and angry with the hand she was dealt. And I was right by her side. I felt called to care for her, and I dug my heels into the ground and did it—when she wanted me to and when she didn't want me to.

And when we reached Bethlehem, I kept caring for

her. I went out into the fields and got us food—when it was hot outside, when it was wet, when it was not fun. I kept going, following what I was called to do, no matter what and no matter the conditions. I thank God that I did reap a reward and my destiny helped to shape history. But what would have happened if I would have given up when it was hard?

Reaching your destiny is not a sprint. It is a long distance run, and it can take your lifetime. You've got to be in it for the long haul to produce what God has destined for you to bring about. If you tap into your passions and follow them with all of your heart—even when you are tired and it feels like forever—you can reach the mark God has set for you.

The journey toward Destiny is like a long distance race, and endurance is the key. Working toward your destiny is a daily endeavor, but every moment won't be filled with thrills or even challenges. Some days are just clocking hours of putting in the work. But when you know why you're working, why you're sacrificing, or why you're delaying gratification, you can sustain your passion for where you are going, especially when that goal seems far away.

Sometimes, we feel like we don't have anything else to give, even to Destiny. During those times especially, it takes determination to continue operating in the day-to-day while keeping a healthy focus on Destiny. When you feel like giving up, take time to review your "why" and your purpose. Envision the goal and recommit to reaching it. Pray for strength, reach out to mentors who are living their destiny, take a deep breath, and keep pressing forward. Your reward will come. You will reach your goal. Your life will be fulfilled, and others will be blessed. It's your destiny.

My Lord, My Rock: Give me a renewed sense of purpose when I get weary. Remind me of what you are calling me to and why. Help me fulfill my destiny.

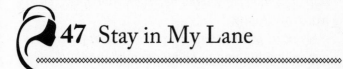

47 Stay in My Lane

And again they wept together, and Orpah kissed her mother-in-law good-bye. But Ruth clung tightly to Naomi. "Look," Naomi said to her, "your sister-in-law has gone back to her people and to her gods. You should do the same."

Ruth 1:14-15 (NLT)

When some people hear about my story—how I stuck with my mother-in-law and journeyed to Bethlehem with her—they ask: What made you stick with her? Why didn't you turn away like Orpah? My answer is simple. I was called to live my own authentic life. I had to do what I thought was right for me. I had to listen to my own destiny calling me on my own path. I can't speak for Orpah or her destiny, but I knew what I was called to do, and I had to do it—no matter what anyone else did.

I even went against my mother-in-law's wishes.

She didn't want me hanging with her. She wanted to journey alone and sulk. But no matter what she said, I had to follow my heart and do what I felt was right. I pushed passed her deterrents and moved toward my destiny.

My path was not Orpah's path. Orpah's path was not my path. I had to know my authentic self and be true to myself. I was called to help my mother-in-law, and I lived a fulfilled life. I met my destiny on my path to doing what I knew I should be doing.

O n this road to Destiny, you've got to keep your eyes on your prize and stay in your own lane. It doesn't matter what other people are doing or are not doing. If it's what you should be doing, you better do it to the best of your ability and forget about others. You will only have to answer for yourself: how well have you followed your path toward Destiny? You can try all of your life to live someone else's life, but it just won't work. What works for your neighbor, may not work for you. That's why people who are in tune with their destiny can cheer on others. When you are on your path to Destiny, another person getting a promotion or a new client or a new car doesn't deter you. You know that what they have is for them, not you.

When you are focused on doing what you are called to do—your destiny—you can be fulfilled and happy and content with what you have and with what you are doing. Your gifts and skills flow when you are in your Destiny zone. When you are not, it doesn't matter how much you have and how good it looks, you are not fulfilled. You live with a hole in your soul.

Invest time in getting to know yourself and your purpose. Figure out what you do well and what you are called to do. Then do it—with all you have. While others hopefully take the path they are called to, you can gladly take the path you are directed toward. This is the only way you will be fulfilled. Stay in your lane and do you—very well.

Awesome and Astounding God: I praise you for you have created me uniquely and with a specific purpose. Keep me focused on my path as I desire to live a fulfilled life for your glory.

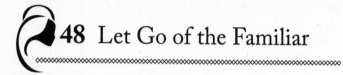48 Let Go of the Familiar

※※

*Strength! Courage! Don't be timid; don't get discouraged. G*OD*,
your God, is with you every step you take."*

Joshua 1:9 (MSG)

When I demanded that my mother-in-law, Naomi,
let me accompany her back to Bethlehem, I didn't
have a clue about the journey or what awaited us
there. Remember, I'm Ruth, a woman from Moab. I
met my husband, Naomi's son, in Moab. His family
had left Bethlehem many years ago trying to escape
a famine. And now all of the men in the family had
died, and we had to decide what to do.

Naomi decided to go back to Bethlehem, and I
chose to go with her. It was a pretty scary thought
to leave my familiar home country and go to a place
where I had never ventured. We really didn't know
how things were there, if the people would welcome

Naomi back, or if they even remembered her. This entire decision required me to step out of my comfort zone and pursue something new.

I put aside my fears—and yes, I had many fears—and I picked up courage. I had heard Naomi and her family talk about their God and all of the wonderful things God had done for them. I knew that God would be with us and would protect us. I just felt it deep down inside, and I was ready to forgo my fear and step into something new. I could have stayed in Moab—I still had my family there. I could have probably remarried someone in Moab—I was a relatively young widow. I could have made a comfortable choice, but I was called to do more, so I had to move forward—even into a new and foreign place.

Destiny reveals herself to risk takers—those adventurous souls who are willing to stick more than a toe in the water. Getting into deep water is scary because no matter how careful you are or how skillful your instructor is, there's a possibility that you could drown. Getting into the water is scary because it's cold. But getting in is the only way you will learn to swim. You can't learn hanging on the edge.

Getting to the next level of life works the same way; you will have to step out of what feels secure and comfortable to attain your destiny. I'm not going to say you won't have fears; you will. But you can gain strength and courage from the words spoken by God to Joshua. God promised to be with Joshua, just as God had been with Moses before Joshua. God makes the same promise to us today.

When we are faced with a new opportunity that places us outside of our familiar territory, we should seek God's wisdom and discern if it is a step we should take. When we hear "yes," we shouldn't expect to have no fears or no discomfort. Instead, we should move forward with the fears and step outside of what feels comfortable and familiar. Our destiny is waiting on the other side. We can't let fear keep us from doing what we have been created to do.

Wonderful Counselor: I know you are with me. I know you have promised to never leave me nor forsake me. I walk with this truth and openly embrace the unfamiliar and uncomfortable so that I may get to my destiny.

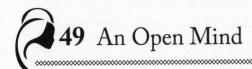

49 An Open Mind

One day Ruth's mother-in-law Naomi said to her, "My daughter, I must find a home for you, where you will be well provided for. Now Boaz, with whose women you have worked, is a relative of ours. Tonight he will be winnowing barley on the threshing floor. Wash, put on perfume, and get dressed in your best clothes."

Ruth 3:1-3 (NIV)

I have been known for stepping out and doing the unthinkable. After all, I did leave my home country and stay by the side of my mother-in-law, Naomi, after my husband had died—and she didn't even want me to travel with her. I could have stayed put and waited around for something else—or someone else—in Moab. But I felt compelled to follow my mother-in-law.

When we made it to Bethlehem and I found us some food, we were doing all right. We probably *could have settled down and enjoyed our time in Bethlehem. But my mother-in-law had another idea—especially once she saw how much grain I was bringing in (Ruth 2). My mother-in-law wanted more for me. She wanted to help me get to my destiny. She suggested I do something uncommon.*

I could have told that old woman to mind her own business and leave me alone. After all, I had already sacrificed for her and I was taking care of her. But I decided to look at things differently. Perhaps Naomi had a good idea. Perhaps something new and exciting and fulfilling could happen if I followed her advice. I put aside my original thoughts and customs and decided to go for it. I did just as Naomi said. I tried something new. And because I was ready to try something new, I got one step closer to my destiny.

Sometimes, gaining a new perspective can help you get what you need to get to your destiny. Open-minded people often examine situations to consider other possibilities or viewpoints that may impact what happens. They are curious about new ideas and perspectives and aren't afraid to try them. Instead of asking what they have to lose by trying something new or thinking a new way, they ask: what do I have to gain? And if the calculated risk seems to be in their favor, they go for it.

A chance encounter with your destiny could be just outside of your window or down the street from your regular stop. If you don't think about venturing out and trying a new place, you might miss out on your destiny. Have an open mind and explore. Listen to other opinions and perspectives. Examine. Pray. Discern. Move forward to your destiny.

My Strong Tower: Give me the insight to try new things and listen to new perspectives. Grant me discernment to know when to move forward.

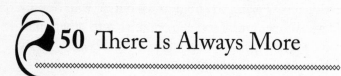

50 There Is Always More

xxxxxxxxxxxxxxxxxxxxxxxxxxxxxxxxxxxxxxxxxxxxxxxxxxxxxxxxxxxxxxxxxxxxxxxxxxxxxxxxx

One day Ruth, the Moabite foreigner, said to Naomi, "I'm going to work; I'm going out to glean among the sheaves, following after some harvester who will treat me kindly." Naomi said, "Go ahead, dear daughter."

Ruth 2:2 (MSG)

I was always looking for more ways to improve my situation as well as my mother-in-law's. After we made it to Bethlehem safely, I knew that wasn't it. We needed to eat, and I needed to continue taking care of her. I wasn't going to rely on anyone else to do it when I was perfectly able to work. I wanted more for us.

And when I found a great place to work, there was still more for me—more food, another relationship, and even more. What would have happened if I would have just given up and assumed that my

situation was permanent? I had had a good mar-
riage with my husband in Moab. I could have been
content and just lived on those memories. I even
had family in Moab. I could have stayed with them
and lived a pretty good life. But I knew there was
more, and I wanted to go after it. I didn't let "this is
it" thinking keep me from my destiny.

Sometimes people think they have seen all they have to see in life and attained all they need to attain. Done it. And then they just stay still and stay in the place they find themselves in, whether that is a good place or not. One of the mistakes the Spaniards made long ago was believing that their land was at the end of the earth. They said: *ne plus ultra*, which means "no more beyond." They inscribed the saying on coins and lived out their beliefs.

When you don't think there is more to where you currently are, you become limited. You think this right here—all I see—is it. This type of thinking keeps you from exploring and discovering. It keeps you from stretching yourself and dreaming about other possibilities. If you want to meet your destiny, you're going to have to believe there is more than what meets the eyes. You're going to have to believe that your vision is limited and trust in God's vision—also known as faith.

You may not be able to see more, but you know there

is more and you live like it. You listen for opportunities. You pray about meetings. You discover new possibilities—all while you hone the gifts you've been given. Destiny followers are always looking to expand—regardless of age, educational level, income, etc. They know that more is beyond, and they commit to scaling barriers or other walls put up by their minds—or by others.

Omnipresent God: I know you are everywhere and you see everything. Increase my faith to see beyond my current situation and to discover my destiny.

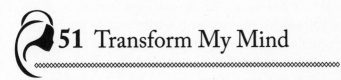

51 Transform My Mind

. . . but let God change the way you think. Then you will know how to do everything that is good and pleasing to him.

Romans 12:2 (CEV)

Culture tells you that mother-in-laws and daughter-in-laws don't care for each other and that they would never talk again once their son/husband died, especially if there were no kids to keep them connected. I didn't follow the cultural norm with my mother-in-law, Naomi. I broke with tradition and decided to renew my mind. I followed what I felt God was telling me to do. I followed what was in my mind.

I didn't want to live a normal life. I wanted to live a fulfilled life. I wanted to live according to God's will for my life. I knew there was more, and I followed what others thought was silly and abnormal. I fol-

lowed what God placed in my heart. It wasn't always easy. Quite frankly, I had to wake up each day and renew my commitment to do as God had called me to do—especially on that long journey back to Bethlehem. For part of it, Naomi was so mad with me that she didn't even talk to me. It took a renewed commitment to do what was in my heart to keep going. But my destiny was calling. I'm glad I answered.

Following the path God has designed for you requires that you shift your mind—sometimes in a way that is counter-cultural. To walk the road toward Destiny, we must transform our minds. The mind, after all, is the steering wheel that determines the direction of one's destiny.

Take some time and make sure your mind is made up; make sure you want to follow God's path. Wake up each morning and ask God to renew your thinking. A renewed mind may need to leave behind conventional thinking and do something others just wouldn't do. A renewed mind will sometimes need to operate based on faith instead of facts.

You limit yourself when you operate only on an intellectual or psychological mode and refuse to pay attention to the spiritual inclinations residing in you. You can turn your mind to education; but somewhere along the line, even a Ph.D. will leave you lacking. You can turn your mind to logic or reason or common sense, or even coincidence, in search of life's answers, but all of these will leave you lacking. Tune in to the fact that the instinct pushing out from you and the purpose pulling at you are a part of God's larger plan for you to fulfill your destiny.

Your mind may guide you in what you do, but the heart affirms your passion to do it; and that leads you to resolve the "why" of your life. Within your passion lies the clue to your deeper purpose—and ultimately, your destiny. As you stand back from yourself to see the push of instincts welded with the pull of purpose that leads you to Destiny, you will know that the events and circumstances in your life equate to more than coincidences or mere facts.

The coming together of all these experiences and connections, some seemingly random, are the result of divine orchestration to empower you to accomplish what God has placed you here to do. And it starts with a renewed mind to follow God's lead and forgo cultural norms.

God of My Mind and Soul: Guide me in the way you would have me to go. Help me to pay attention to the

prickling in my heart and renew my mind daily to follow you instead of what is popular.

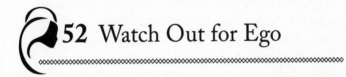

52 Watch Out for Ego

×××

First pride, then the crash— the bigger the ego, the harder the fall.
It's better to live humbly among the poor than to live it up among
the rich and famous. It pays to take life seriously; things work out
when you trust in GOD.

Proverbs 16:18-20 (MSG)

My ego would have let me kiss Naomi good-bye and send her off on her way to Bethlehem. I still had family in Moab. I could have stayed with them and made a decent life for myself. If my ego would have gotten its way, I would not have stood up to my mother-in-law and supported her on her journey back to Bethlehem. My decision to do right wasn't easy—mainly because of Naomi's attitude.

My mother-in-law was bitter (Ruth 1:20). I'm not judging her; after all, she had been through a lot and she felt empty and hopeless. Her attitude af-

fected how she treated me. She didn't want me to make this journey with her; she preferred to be left alone to sulk and remain bitter. She wasn't into having a young woman return to Bethlehem beside her. I sucked it up, put up with her bad attitude, and journeyed with her to Bethlehem and toward my destiny. I'm glad I let my ego go and focused on what I knew was right.

Decisions. Decisions. Decisions. We all have to make them when we are on the road toward Destiny. One thing I've seen get in the way of people making good decisions is their ego. When you let your ego get out of control, it will make you mad and irrational. It will make you ask questions like: How dare he do that to me? How dare she say that to me? What do they expect? Even though there may be good and reasonable times to ask these questions, there are times when we have to discern when to move on and keep marching toward Destiny.

If you are purpose-minded, you won't let ego trips stop you from reaching your destiny. You will be able to identify when pride is rearing its ugly head and command it to back down. You have a greater task at hand, and you don't have room for false pride.

Many times the issues at hand are other people's issues, much like Naomi not wanting Ruth to journey with her. Learn to seek wisdom before you lash out because of your pride. Learn to rely on and trust in God to be your compass as you navigate toward your destiny.

My God: Thank you for reminding me to rely on you every step of the way. Put my ego in check each time it threatens to rear its ugly head. I desire to live according to your will, not my own.

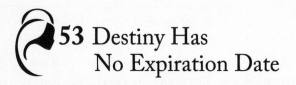

53 Destiny Has No Expiration Date

〰〰〰〰〰〰〰〰〰〰〰〰〰〰〰〰〰〰〰〰〰〰〰〰〰〰〰〰〰〰〰〰〰〰〰

"Then, after doing all those things, I will pour out my Spirit upon all people. Your sons and daughters will prophesy. Your old men will dream dreams, and your young men will see visions. In those days I will pour out my Spirit even on servants—men and women alike."

Joel 2:28-29 (NLT)

Then the women of the town said to Naomi, "Praise the LORD, who has now provided a redeemer for your family! May this child be famous in Israel. May he restore your youth and care for you in your old age. For he is the son of your daughter-in-law who loves you and has been better to you than seven sons!"

Ruth 4:14-15 (NLT)

Even though I thought life had ended for me, I soon found out that Destiny has no expiration date. By journeying with my daughter-in-law, Ruth, I (Nao-

mi) learned that you're never too old to live a fulfilling life.

When my husband died and then both of my sons died, I thought my life was over. What was an old, single woman to do? What did I have to look forward to? I felt barren and fruitless and like I had nothing to contribute to society.

I learned to love my daughter-in-law as much as she loved me. She was a loyal and lovely young woman who journeyed back to my home country with me—although she didn't have any reason to do so. And then she took such good care of me; she went to the fields and worked hard so we could have food to eat. God blessed me with Ruth. And if that wasn't enough, God led Ruth to the field of one of our relatives, Boaz. When I noticed how kind he was to dear Ruth, I had to intervene and help her to let Boaz know she was interested and available.

If only I had known what God had in store; Boaz and Ruth did get married, and they had a son. I got to take care of him. Some way, somehow, God replaced my emptiness with a full life—filled with family and a baby boy, too. My Destiny didn't die when my husband and sons died. I still had life to live. I still had love to give.

As long as you have life in your body, God is able to turn any situation around and restore what you have lost. An important lesson to learn—especially for those who feel they are in the twilight season of life—is that Destiny has no expiration date. In *Destiny*, I tell about renowned journalist Bob Schaeffer who told me one of his greatest accomplishments occurred after the age of 65. His testimony reminded me to not let age deter my move forward.

You can still dream dreams, no matter your age. Scripture reminds us that God has the ability to pour out God's Spirit on young and old, and do new things in young people and in old people. Don't let your age deter you from continuing your journey toward your destiny. You're going to have to live this life anyway. Why not live it while fulfilling your purpose and grasping your destiny? Who knows what a difference you can make and what a legacy you might leave.

I also tell the story of a woman who bemoaned the fact that she had not finished college. Her friend asked her what was stopping her from going back and getting her degree. The woman shared that she felt too old; she was currently forty-eight years old, and it would take her at least six years to finish her degree while going to school part time. She would be fifty-four years old and just getting her degree. Her wise companion then asked her, "Well, how old will you be in six years if you don't go back to school?" I'm sure the woman got it: she'd be fifty-four whether she pursued her dream or not. When you know you have not gone as far as Destiny wants you to go, age is little more than a number.

Keep dreaming. Keep moving forward.

Spirit of the Living God: Breathe fresh on me. I want to dream again. Restore my vision so I may see the destiny you have planned for me.

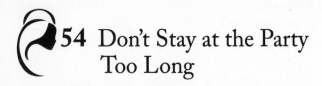

54 Don't Stay at the Party Too Long

×××

The LORD says, "I will guide you along the best pathway for your life. I will advise you and watch over you."

Psalm 32:8 (NLT)

It had been comforting to stay in a place I knew. But I understood that my time in Moab had come to an end. My husband had died. I was ready to move when God said move because I knew things in Moab had ended. I wasn't sure how things in Bethlehem would work out, but I knew God would be right by my and Naomi's side. I trusted God to send new provisions to reach my goal.

Have you ever had a party guest refuse to leave? You start to clean up, you turn off the music, you might even dim the lights, but this person is still at your home, thinking the party is still going on. You actually might have to ask this person to leave because they just don't realize that everyone else has left and you're trying to get to bed.

Some people act like that party guest when pursuing their destiny. They refuse to hear that the music has ended. They refuse to look around them and see that things have changed and that they need to move in another direction. While their vision is still the same, the provisions God is using to bring about that vision have changed. And now, in order to reach the goal, the person will have to employ new tactics and venture on a new path.

Change is not easy. Don't allow your fear of moving and changing get in the way of your destiny. You don't want to be the last one at the party before you realize it is over. This is where it is important to keep your eyes open and your heart open to what God is doing in your life and in the world.

Rely on God to show you when to change and move— and then go forth without fear. Be ready to release a provision that has reached its end. Your next party just might be in another location, in another relationship, in another time zone.

Great Jehovah: Forgive me for staying too long when I know my time had ended. I desire to follow your path and your will for my life. I only want to be where you want me to be.

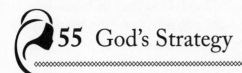# 55 God's Strategy

*"My thoughts are nothing like your thoughts," says the LORD.
"And my ways are far beyond anything you could imagine.*
Isaiah 55:8 (NLT)

There were a few times during my journey with Naomi that I could have just stopped. I could have turned around and ran back home—if I was following my own thoughts. Naomi was not the nicest woman or the most gracious companion—and to top it off, she was my deceased husband's mother. I didn't have to stay with her when she insulted me, refused to talk to me, and treated me badly. But thank God I knew better, and I could rely on God's strategy, not my own.

Throughout this journey God kept pushing me and urging me to be faithful to my mother-in-law. I had no idea what God had in store for me.

When you really decide to live a complete and full life, following the path God has designed just for you, you're going to need to stick very close to God. God can't be boxed into a plan or figured out like a puzzle. You've got to trust and believe and follow—even when things seem crazy. And you've got to rely on God instead of human nature to keep going and to pursue the strategy God gives you.

Be open to listening to God. The collaborative nature of working with God means that you cannot call all of the shots nor can you fit God into a formula. How and what God did yesterday—or for someone else today—is not necessarily the way God will work in your situation. Through faith and trust, you learn to lean on God and look for God's cues. They can come through the infomercial you're stuck watching at 3 a.m. because you can't sleep, or they can come from a stranger you've just met. Your cues may come through a still voice, through a Scripture, or through another story. Be open. Be attentive. Believe that God hears and sees you and wants to match you up with your destiny.

Through your internal strategy, you can make moves that will get you closer to Destiny. By tuning into your internal compass, you can resist the urge to act rationally and forgo a great opportunity just because you are insulted. Your internal strategy and compass keeps you focused on the forest, not just the trees. Your internal strategy keeps you focused on the picture you are creating with God.

God, My Navigator: Lead me and guide me in the way I should go. Help me to ignore my human desires and focus on your leading. I know what you have planned is far better than I can imagine.

56 Serendipity Plus Preparation

〰〰

One day Naomi said to Ruth, "My daughter, it's time that I found a permanent home for you, so that you will be provided for. Boaz is a close relative of ours, and he's been very kind by letting you gather grain with his young women. Tonight he will be winnowing barley at the threshing floor. Now do as I tell you—take a bath and put on perfume and dress in your nicest clothes. Then go to the threshing floor, but don't let Boaz see you until he has finished eating and drinking. Be sure to notice where he lies down; then go and uncover his feet and lie down there. He will tell you what to do."

"I will do everything you say," Ruth replied. So she went down to the threshing floor that night and followed the instructions of her mother-in-law.

Ruth 3:1-6 (NLT)

When you read my story of how I met Boaz, you might think that I got lucky. After all, I happened upon the right field when I went out to look for food for my mother-in-law and me (see Ruth 2). But let me tell you, luck is not what helped me to reach my destiny. It might seem like serendipity led me to the right field, but I like to call it: God ordering my steps.

And even then I had to be ready and prepared for God to show me the right place and the right time to make my move. I had done a lot to prepare for this moment. I had followed Naomi back to her hometown. I had made up my mind that I was able-bodied and could go out and work to take care of us. I was in the right position, and I listened to Naomi's wise counsel.

God can make that serendipitous moment line up when you listen to the right counsel, like I did with Naomi. I could have waited around for my luck to get better, but I put my hands to work. I went into the fields, and I just so happened to be in the right one. I listened to Naomi and received her instructions well.

There's a lot of talk in some church circles about being anointed. It's a way of acknowledging a person's destiny. But, too often, I've seen this concept distorted into an exemption from hard work and sacrifice. God can position you in places where the odds say you would never be, but the positioning comes after preparation.

None of us is exempt from getting training, acquiring knowledge, paying dues, or gaining experience. You still need preparation, no matter how much anointing you have. The same principle applies to natural talent. Preparation—formal or informal—is a prerequisite for Destiny. Some people get what they need from attending great institutions of higher learning. But other people gain their preparation in the school of life—those are the ups and downs that toughen us, strengthen us, and give us wisdom for what lies ahead.

No matter how talented you are, how lucky you are, or how strong your anointing is, you must be willing to do what is necessary to reach your destiny. The actions required of you may be difficult, they may be uncomfortable, and they will be challenging; but your God-directed strategy will get you there. Preparation may take longer than you'd hope or planned, but keep going until you are face-to-face with success.

There really is no such thing as an overnight success. All of the people we consider to be successful—whether on television or in movies or in the community, or even in the pulpit—all have paid dues to get there. It takes serendipity plus preparation.

In this journey, you've got to have both—training and a serendipity that I believe can be orchestrated only by God.

Divine Director: Thank you for ordering my steps toward my destiny. I will honor you and show my gratitude by preparing and training so I can be ready for every opportunity you orchestrate.

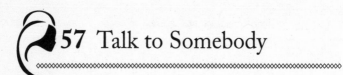

57 Talk to Somebody

The empty-headed treat life as a plaything; the perceptive grasp its meaning and make a go of it. Refuse good advice and watch your plans fail; take good counsel and watch them succeed. Congenial conversation—what a pleasure! The right word at the right time—beautiful!

Proverbs 15:21-23 (MSG)

As I think about my journey, I now realize that Naomi was a part of my destiny from the beginning. I'm glad I listened to her wise counsel when she told me to approach Boaz. I really didn't know exactly how things would work out, but I followed her instructions to the letter (see Ruth 3).

I wasn't going to just listen to any older person, but I had been around Naomi and I observed how people respected her. She had lived an exemplary life, and she could share her experiences with me.

I trusted her thoughts, I trusted her advice, and I knew she had my best interest in mind. I had taken care of us, and now she wanted to take care of me. Yes, I listened to her and did exactly what she said to do. This wise one knew what she was talking about, and our plans succeeded. We both were able to meet our destiny and live joyous lives.

God is our main Helper who will call and then lead us to our destiny; but it's critical to have at least one human being who can guide you on this journey, too. Listening to a wise mentor and learning from the experiences of others in pursuit of Destiny can boost you past the mistakes you may make while trying to do everything on your own. You need someone in your life who has successfully navigated the territory you're trying to cross. You need a trusted mentor.

I often suggest that people find someone who has already crossed the path they are on. For example, if you are a husband struggling to finish college courses and spend time with your family, talk to someone who has been down that path before. Talk to a successful business owner who had to file bankruptcy after the first business failure or someone who became a success despite flunking out of college or despite a prison record. No one has a perfect journey to Destiny, and talking with a mentor who has experience can help you realize that there's nothing wrong with you—and that person could provide insight into a breakthrough like Naomi did for Ruth. Your mentor could provide the right word at the right time to make all of the difference on your journey.

Wonderful Counselor: I need help on this journey. Help me to identify mentors that I can trust and listen to.

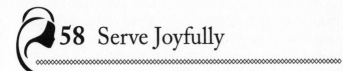

58 Serve Joyfully

Above all, maintain constant love for one another, for love covers a multitude of sins. Be hospitable to one another without complaining. Like good stewards of the manifold grace of God, serve one another with whatever gift each of you has received.

1 Peter 4:8-10 (NRSV)

I sometimes wonder how my story would have turned out if I hadn't befriended my mother-in-law, let go of my ego, and humbly served her during her time of need. I wonder if Naomi would have been as open with me if I hadn't served her first.

The lesson I learned is: Serve. Serve. Serve. While I didn't accompany Naomi to Bethlehem to be paid back nor did I go out in the field and get us food so she would return the favor, I do think she was much more open to caring for me and sharing with me because of how I had already served her.

I t's always best to serve in love and to be humble. You never know who may bless you in return. When you are pursuing the help of a mentor, it's important to remember that you are in a new circle and you will more than likely need to forget about status and recognition. You may be lauded in the circle you came from, but you may have to serve in this one. In short, humility is the key to entering new levels.

The question I am most often asked by people when the topic of mentoring comes up is, "How do I gain access to people who are doing what I would love to do?" Our late president, John F. Kennedy, defined it best in the statement, "Ask not what your country can do for you, but what you can do for your country." In principle, Kennedy was saying what all mentees must understand. Your needs aren't as attractive to busy people as their own. What you can get from them is not their primary concern, so the relationship should be focused on seeking opportunities to add value to those you want to glean from. In the process of giving what you have, you will gain what you do not. It is better to be a doorkeeper to your future than to be a prince of your past!

So humble yourself and keep your prospective mentor's interest in focus when asking questions. Remember that most people really enjoy talking about themselves and the things that concern them. Their personal journey is often what they are most passionate about. Employ this three-fold philosophy and begin a dialog with a potential mentor by saying, "I am amazed at how you do this!" instead of "I don't know how to do this." The mentor's point of interest is often not as effective when it begins with you. Seek to find out about them, seek ways to serve them, and you'll reap unforeseen benefits.

Almighty and Amazing God: Give me an attitude to serve my mentors and others. Open doors that will give me access to new levels so that I may continue the journey that you have called me to.

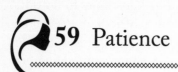

59 Patience

Finishing is better than starting. Patience is better than pride.
Ecclesiastes 7:8 (NLT)

I grew so much during my journey that I can now look back and see how everything I went through was helping me develop into the person who could handle my destiny (Ruth 1). Through this journey, I picked up so many lessons that taught me to be patient, to trust God, and to keep going.

When I married Boaz and we had a child, I was a different person than the young girl back in Moab. By that time, I was a believer in the process of God. By that time, I had learned the beauty of caring for another person simply because you think it is your calling—not for personal gain or attention or through pity. I was able to use all of those lessons when I was called to raise the grandfather of King

David, who would also be the forefather of the Savior. What a destiny I was charged to meet and fulfill. I'm thankful God prepared me.

In *Destiny*, I tell the story about a speech then-senator Barack Obama gave to a group of college students; he offered these sage words about success: "Focusing your life solely on making a buck shows a certain poverty of ambition. It asks too little of yourself. Because it's only when you hitch your wagon to something larger than yourself that you realize your true potential."

Purpose is bigger than ego and can sustain you as you travel Destiny's path. Identify your purpose, and then let patience perfect you! Patience purges bad motives and clears jealous vision. It allows you to mature and increases clarity. Patience helps you learn the lessons you need to pass the tests of life and keep growing and going toward your destiny.

Powerful Purpose-Giver: I want to keep going and growing, learning all that you would have me to know on this journey. Give me the spirit to patiently walk on this journey toward my destiny.

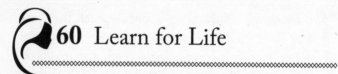60 Learn for Life

xxxxxxxxxxxxxxxxxxxxxxxxxxxxxxxxxxxxxxxxxxxxxxxxxxxxxxxxxxxxxxxxxxxxxxxxxxxxxxxxx

Then the way you live will always honor and please the Lord, and your lives will produce every kind of good fruit. All the while, you will grow as you learn to know God better and better. We also pray that you will be strengthened with all his glorious power so you will have all the endurance and patience you need.

Colossians 1:10-11 (NLT)

When my husband and sons died, I (Naomi, Ruth's mother-in-law) was devastated. I was angry and bitter. How could I be so full one day and so empty the next? My family was my life. I lived for them. When my family died, I felt like my life had ended, too.

Although I felt abandoned, I now realize God had not left me. God gave me Ruth to walk beside me. I learned from her to not give up even though our circumstances were not optimal. I learned to look for new opportunities to sustain ourselves when re-

sources ran out. I learned to be open to God's provi-
dence because you just never know what's around
the corner.

Who would have thought I could learn so much
from a younger woman? I'm grateful for the journey
with Ruth, my daughter-in-law and my teacher.

Destiny requires a commitment to lifelong learning. No matter how much you think you know, always be willing to take another step of growth toward your destiny.

Failing to grow into new horizons can blind you to the beauty of life's adventures. You become like a plant that's outgrown its container. Have you ever purchased or been given a plant that grew to the confines of its container? When you decide to shift the plant to a larger pot, you may notice that the roots have grown into the shape of the receptacle that holds it. If you hadn't replanted it into something larger, the plant would remain the same size. That happens to people, too. Their growth can be limited to the confines of their environment, and they will grow no further without being taken to a new arena.

Is Destiny beckoning you somewhere? This could mean a new physical location, or it could mean a new spiritual level or emotional space. Be open to hearing God calling you to new places—and be committed to following and venturing into different arenas. Destiny awaits you.

Omnipresent Lord: I know you are everywhere, so I will not fear moving to new territories and new arenas. I am happy to venture into new places and to learn new lessons on this journey toward my destiny.

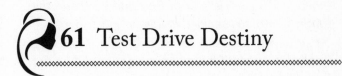

61 Test Drive Destiny

Taste and see that the LORD is good. Oh, the joys of those who take refuge in him! Fear the LORD, you his godly people, for those who fear him will have all they need. Even strong young lions sometimes go hungry, but those who trust in the LORD will lack no good thing.

Psalm 34:8-10 (NLT)

I could have played life safely, but I would not have reaped the same benefits if I had. There were opportunities on the journey when I could have decided not to go after the unfamiliar; I could have decided to choose the same old, same old. But that wasn't me, and I'm glad I tested different arenas and became exposed to people and things that I was not used to.

From the beginning, I went against the grain and married an Israelite man (Naomi's son) even though

I was from Moab. And I was open to my husband's culture. I even adopted Naomi's God when I decided to follow her back to Bethlehem (Ruth 1). I had listened to their stories about God and had seen the family's faith, so I decided to follow God, too.

I also was exposed to seeking help when you needed it—even if it was unconventional. I hadn't heard of going to the threshing floor to let a man know you were available for marriage, but I tried it. I trusted Naomi; and by this time, I was used to trying new and different things. I thought: My exposure to the new has served me well thus far; why stop trying now? This is how I lived the rest of my Destiny journey—never afraid to try something new or be exposed to something different. It made life exciting.

Have the attitude that exposure cannot hurt you; it's your test drive to Destiny. Gaining exposure is like test driving a car. You enter a new arena and you see if it fits. You see what it costs you to be in that environment, and determine whether you want to pay the price.

Marvelous Maker: I am in awe of your magnificent plans. I know you will not hold back any good thing

from me. I want to joyfully embrace all of the new things and ideas you have designed for me.

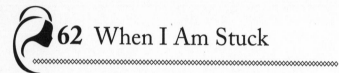

62 When I Am Stuck

"Don't call me Naomi," she responded. "Instead, call me Mara, for the Almighty has made life very bitter for me. I went away full, but the LORD has brought me home empty. Why call me Naomi when the LORD has caused me to suffer and the Almighty has sent such tragedy upon me?"

Ruth 1:20–21 (NLT)

When my mother-in-law, Naomi, was dealing with the deaths of her husband and then her sons, she was in a bad place. She didn't even know her true name; she didn't want people calling her by the name her parents had bestowed on her. She was not herself. I had to encourage her to get unstuck and keep going. Because I encouraged her to keep going, she found enough resolve to move forward. She found a way to help me, too. When she heard that I had been in Boaz's field, she slowly got a little more *life in her.*

She had a project now, and she started to move into action. My mother-in-law learned and kept going.

Sometimes when you have lost the things you once knew and loved, you have to keep your eyes open for the new. You have to look for new challenges and new things to give you hope and purpose. When we are unable to move with the flow of Destiny or when the flow changes and we refuse to travel with it, we may find that we can no longer enjoy what used to bring us pleasure. We can't laugh at the things that we used to find funny. We become dissatisfied with the things that used to bring contentment.

Life has many wonderful opportunities that do not come to us because of foreknowledge or by any planning on our part. We must learn to go with the flow, even when it feels as if God has stirred up what once brought us assurance and peace. Destiny requires that we move on.

God, My Rock and My Strength: When the bottom falls out, I know you still have a plan for me. Give me strength to get up and look for the new.

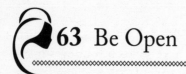# 63 Be Open

One day Ruth the Moabite said to Naomi, "Let me go out into the harvest fields to pick up the stalks of grain left behind by anyone who is kind enough to let me do it." Naomi replied, "All right, my daughter, go ahead.

Ruth 2:2 (NLT)

Just as you cannot understand the path of the wind or the mystery of a tiny baby growing in its mother's womb, so you cannot understand the activity of God, who does all things. Plant your seed in the morning and keep busy all afternoon, for you don't know if profit will come from one activity or another—or maybe both.

Ecclesiastes 11:5-6 (NLT)

When I set out to get food for my mother-in-law and myself, I had no idea what I'd find in the fields. I had heard that the harvesting field was not always a safe place for a woman to be, but I knew I needed to take care of Naomi and we needed food. So I tried *something new. I didn't have to go out and get my own food when I was living in Moab with my husband; even after he died, we had provisions made for us in Moab. But I had decided to venture out of my comfort zone and go to Bethlehem with Naomi. This was all so very new for me.*

When I went out that morning seeking grain for us, I had no idea I'd stumble across the fields of a relative. But it happened because I stepped out and did something new. I tried on a new role. I did something different. And I met my destiny. I didn't know my story would turn out the way it did; I couldn't have dreamt it up in a million years.

While I extol the positive outcomes of exposure and the need for it, I remind you that exposure can also help you know what you don't want. You may want to be famous; but when you open your eyes and become exposed to the reality of fame, you may realize that you prefer the freedom that comes with being unknown better than the popularity of fame. Or you may think you want to own your own business; but when you are exposed to the realities of entrepreneurship, you realize that having a paycheck every two weeks better suits your budget and spending needs. Exposure can help you know where you fit or do not fit.

That said, give the new arena time before you decide whether or not it's a fit for you. First impressions may be based on faulty or incomplete information. And jump in with a sense of adventure. You have lots to learn from your new place—whether you decide to stay or leave. Who knows what or who you will meet that could change your life forever.

Omniscient God: Give me a sense of adventure each day so that I may welcome exposure and new opportunities. Give me discernment to know how long to stay in each place to which you guide me.

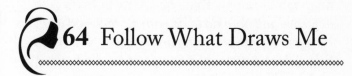

64 Follow What Draws Me

Steep your life in God-reality, God-initiative, God-provisions. Don't worry about missing out. You'll find all your everyday human concerns will be met.

Matthew 6:33 (MSG)

I am famous. After all, I have a book of the Bible named after me (Ruth). But fame is not what I set out to obtain. That's not how you get to your destiny—chasing after fame or fortune. I got to my destiny by doing what I felt called to do—plain and simply. I had no idea taking care of my poor, widowed mother-in-law would lead me to being hailed in the story of King David and eventually our Savior. Who would have thought that a lowly girl from a foreign country, who just felt passionately about not sending her mother-in-law back to Bethlehem alone, would be talked about throughout time?

I'm glad God allowed me to see more than I had seen and to become more than I had dreamed; but it all began with me following the inner urging to take care of Naomi. Fame had nothing to do with it. Riches had nothing to do with it. I followed what I knew to be true and right, and I was faithful. That's how I met up with my destiny and lived a fulfilled, and notable, life.

Economic, commercial, and professional successes are ancillary to the journey to Destiny. Follow what you believe in and enjoy. Do not start on a quest to figure out the quickest way to fame and wealth. That's a critical point about Destiny. Yours may include fame, but fame is not the purpose of Destiny.

Seek your destiny. Do not join the throng of thousands trying to be famous because they love fame—because of the adulation and attention that it brings. Those who have enjoyed enduring fame never sought fame for fame's sake. They were following a dream or a vision to accomplish something that drew them. Follow their example.

Follow what draws you, and watch fulfillment follow you. God has a special way of taking care of those who follow the path God has set for them. Follow God's vision and be fulfilled.

Provider and Positioner: I commit to following your path for my life. I will not focus on getting rich or famous, but on doing what you have called me to do. I am grateful.

65 Pursue Courage

For GOD's Word is solid to the core; everything he makes is sound inside and out.

Psalm 33:4 (MSG)

I had to muster up some courage to follow the path I was called toward. When my mother-in-law told me to go and do the unthinkable—pursue Boaz— I wasn't really sure how things would work out. I didn't know if I'd get thrown out or if I'd be the talk of the town, but I needed to be courageous. I needed to go and grasp what was meant for me—and I had to do it. I couldn't sit by and idly wait or wish for things to happen; my effort was needed. I mustered up enough courage and went to Boaz. I met my destiny when I got up and went for it.

Following the path toward Destiny takes some guts; it's not for the faint-hearted. Be courageous enough to pursue Destiny. Stand up in this world occupied by more than seven billion people and say, "I have a unique purpose and a destiny that is distinct from any other person who has ever lived." Know that you have a role, an idea, a plan, or a vision to make a contribution to humanity. You have been created for Destiny.

Have the courage to be uniquely you, to be different. It is easier and less stressful *not* to be successful, to be mediocre, *not* to make waves. No courage is required to be normal and fit in. If you are more concerned about people's opinion of you than God's vision for you, then neutralize what the Almighty created in you, give in to peer pressure, and fit in with everyone else. Dress like them. Act like them. Eat what they eat. Spend seventy hours a week watching television like they do. Live on credit, or check to check, like they do, satisfied with barely getting by. Overspend like them. Go where they go. Think like they think. Talk like they talk.

Neutralize your divinely-created uniqueness and you won't need courage. In this reality TV society that we live in today where the weak, watered-down, and me-diocre is the standard, it takes courage to say, "I didn't come through all that I've been through to fit a definition of normalcy. I have the courage to go after my dream!" Be courageous enough to claim your right and affirm your ability to rise to greater heights. You're a rising star. You have inside you the courage and stamina to push away the negativity of conformity. Invite Destiny to come in.

Mighty God: Give me the courage and strength to go after my destiny. I desire to live the life you've created me to live.

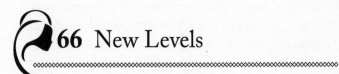

66 New Levels

Naomi took the baby and held him in her arms, cuddling him, cooing over him, waiting on him hand and foot. The neighborhood women started calling him "Naomi's baby boy!" But his real name was Obed. Obed was the father of Jesse, and Jesse the father of David.

Ruth 4:16-17 (MSG)

I learned from my mother-in-law, especially, that God always has new places and new levels for you, no matter what your situation looks like now. Some people might think that Naomi was in the twilight of her life; she had married, raised her boys, and lived her life. She had even reluctantly served as my mentor and taught me a lot about living in all seasons of life. She showed me how to pick up and move when doors had closed; she showed me how to go after

*what I wanted and to be bold. She showed me how
to grieve.*

*But God showed me something through Naomi—
and that was a reminder that there is always more.
There is always another level to attain when you are
living this life. Naomi may have seemed like a settled
woman who had seen the world and lived through
the ups and downs; but God wasn't through with
her yet. Her destiny had not come to an end. God
gave her more and even more purpose.*

*After she helped me marry Boaz, we had a child.
And she helped me raise my child. She was not only
a mentor and midwife who helped me bear part of
my destiny; she also helped my son and received
joy through him. It wasn't over for Naomi. She had
more levels to get to.*

At no stage of life should you be content to sit comfortably, thinking that you have arrived or that Destiny offers no new vistas of opportunity, challenge, or growth for you. There is always another level to attain in some arena of life.

God has created us humans as fascinating creatures that are able to grow on many different levels. You may have reached your highest economic destiny, but you have not yet arrived at your highest level spiritually. You may still have room to grow to a level where you tune out the world's chatter to hear the voice of God speaking to you. You may have reached your professional destiny, but still have room to grow in your personal journey.

Look around and see where God is leading you. New opportunities lie ahead—things you may or may not have ever considered. Don't stop at this level. Keep moving and growing and learning. Destiny always has more.

Great and Mighty God: Thank you for taking me to new levels. I vow to keep reaching for your very best in my life so that I may glorify you.

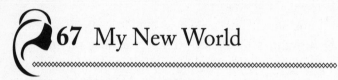

67 My New World

So Ruth did it—she stuck close to Boaz's young women, gleaning in the fields daily until both the barley and wheat harvesting were finished. And she continued living with her mother-in-law.

Ruth 2:23 (MSG)

I learned very early on my journey to try new things—to become comfortable with new people, new customs, and new experiences. I married a man who was not from my country, and I even ventured to his country with his mother (Naomi) after our husbands died. I'm thankful that God helped me embrace the new—the new location in Bethlehem, the new role in caring for Naomi, and the new family in meeting Boaz and producing an heir. New was not foreign to me and I wasn't afraid of new—that's part of the way I reached my destiny.

If you're going to go after your destiny, you will be wise to learn to be comfortable around the new. Not everyone will come with you at each leg of your journey; it's just not the way of Destiny. So if you want to remain as you are and stay with the same people and in the same places, you're not going to grow or go very far.

Destiny requires an adventurous spirit and a realization that things change, new opportunities come, and life moves on. You have to expand with it. If you sit back, you'll let it pass you by. It's important to realize that your old world doesn't belong with your new world.

Walking into your destiny will take you into a new arena and that can sometimes be lonely. As lonely as you may feel at times, remember that your new world is worthy of discovery. Meet the people in it. Savor the new experiences. Find fulfillment in the life Destiny has drawn you into. Your experiences have made you stronger, but they were not meant to define all of your life. Fill your loneliness with the spirit of an explorer. There's so much in your new world that you don't know. The people there may have a different history, but they have overcome their own challenges. You can learn from them, like them, and even find commonalities in your experiences.

Part of the journey toward Destiny is embracing the

new world and the new experiences. Enjoy each moment. Become a tourist of your new world and soak in the sights, people, and new reality. God didn't bring you here to just sit as a bystander; get in there and enjoy your new world. It's your destiny. Embrace the new.

Splendid and Satisfying Savior: Grant me the ability to embrace new experiences, new people, and a new reality. Help me to make the most of each day and each opportunity so that I may live on purpose and in your will.

68 Be Creative

Make a careful exploration of who you are and the work you have been given, and then sink yourself into that. Don't be impressed with yourself. Don't compare yourself with others. Each of you must take responsibility for doing the creative best you can with your own life.

Galatians 6:4-5 (MSG)

My family would have welcomed me into their homes and lives if I had decided to stay put and reside in Moab (Ruth 1). Moab was where my life was. It was really all I knew. So when I felt the urging to move on and follow my mother-in-law to Bethlehem, many didn't understand— even my mother-in-law. Why would a young woman want to go to a foreign land with her mother-in-law when her husband wasn't even alive? I'm sure my family thought I had lost my mind. They had never heard of such a *thing—loyalty to an in-law even when your spouse was dead.*

But when I made the decision to escape my comfort zone and what was considered "normal," I made the decision to live my best life and to be creative and open to what God had in store for me. It wasn't always an easy decision to go against the grain, but it paid off. I found my destiny by leaving my familiar and venturing into the unfamiliar.

When you're focused on your own path, your mind is open to new ideas and revelations. Your limitless potential can be shaped by Destiny's unfettered hand. Those who avoid the lure of creativity are residents of the comfort zone.

Those who like safety inhabit the comfort zone. The comfort zone is the land of *laissez-faire,* whose language is: "We've never done it that way before." Those words stop progress, stifle creativity, halt innovation. Life in the comfort zone requires no challenge, no guts, and no determination. Everyone who lives in the comfort zone is expected to speak like others speak, do what others do, and not do what others don't do. They choke creativity down to what they can understand.

The comfort zone looks easygoing, but it's tense and controlling. Residents of the comfort zone demand total allegiance. You can't live among them and dare to be different. You can't zip into the comfort zone, and then move out of it when you get a burst of creativity. You'll be punished for trying to live among them while they perceive you are simultaneously betraying them with your new ideas and originality.

If you're going to intentionally pursue your destiny, you're going to have to decide in which zone you will reside: comfort or creativity. Don't be afraid to move forward and think outside of the box. It's where new ideas are found.

Bountiful Lord: I want to live this life on the creative side, open to new possibilities and adventures. Give me the wisdom and discernment to know when and where to move.

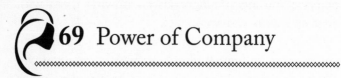69 Power of Company

As iron sharpens iron, so one person sharpens another.

Proverbs 27:17 (NIV)

By yourself you're unprotected. With a friend you can face the worst. Can you round up a third? A three-stranded rope isn't easily snapped.

Ecclesiastes 4:12 (MSG)

When Naomi and I started on this journey back to Bethlehem, no one could possibly guess how our lives would turn out. No one could predict that we would help each other reach our destiny and set into motion a world-changing succession plan for the kingdom of God.

Naomi and I learned to work together; it could have been that long journey to Bethlehem, or it could have been the countless days and hours we spent together getting by on leftover wheat. We eventually helped each other grow and expand and make room for new things in our lives. We sharpened each other. I learned from Naomi, and Naomi learned from me. My life was better because I was in company with her; her life was better because of our connection. For us, two was better than one. We found strength from each other.

Finding your creative zone doesn't mean you sing or paint or sculpt or write or display any talents customarily defined as creative. The creative zone is simply the place where your unchartered journey to Destiny is free to explore all roads.

Whatever your revealed purpose, you will be energized by opening your mind to ideas, and closing the narrow mental corridors of convention and sameness. Look for people who are also on the path toward Destiny and collaborate with them; you can gain strength from each other's vision and thirst to follow Destiny. As you find your way out of the safety of sameness, you will link up with creative comrades who make you better as you make them better.

Innovative God: I desire to walk with those who also

want to follow their destiny. Show me the people who will strengthen my vision and energize me.

70 Engage My Best Self

xxxxxxxxxxxxxxxxxxxxxxxxxxxxxxxxxxxxxxxxxxxxxxxxxxxxxxxxxxxxxxxxxxxxxxxxxxx

Concentrate on doing your best for God, work you won't be ashamed of, laying out the truth plain and simple.

2 Timothy 2:15 (MSG)

On my route toward my journey, I sometimes got tired and weary; there were even some moments when I wanted to give up. When I signed up to accompany Naomi back to her homeland, I made a vow to her and I made a vow to God. This wasn't about me. It was about keeping my word to her and, most importantly, keeping my word to God. So when I got tired and weary, I stopped and asked God to renew me. I stopped and refocused on the big picture—pleasing God.

Each time, my desire to please God re-energized me and gave me the extra boost I needed to make it over the hump. I sincerely wanted to do my best for

God. It's how I reached my destiny.

Life has much to offer, and pursuing your destiny can be exciting and thrilling. But it also requires your entire being. Destiny chasers engage every fiber of their being in following the path God has set before them. They are not bored or lazy or negative—and when they find themselves displaying these behaviors, they have to check themselves. They have to remind themselves why they are on this journey.

When you want to be your best and do your best for God, you keep moving past the humps. You find the energy to re-engage in your purpose, and you remember that your calling is greater than you.

Precious Lord: I need you to re-energize me when I am weary. Remind me to keep moving forward because reaching my destiny is not just about me. I have a greater purpose.

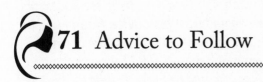

71 Advice to Follow

Oh, the joys of those who do not follow the advice of the wicked, or stand around with sinners, or join in with mockers. But they delight in the law of the LORD, meditating on it day and night. They are like trees planted along the riverbank, bearing fruit each season. Their leaves never wither, and they prosper in all they do.

Psalm 1:1-3 (NLT)

I trusted my mother-in-law, Naomi. That is why I was able to follow her unconventional advice and approach Boaz. I had received my share of good and bad advice along my journey. Some people told me not to go follow after Naomi when she wanted to leave Moab. Others told me to find a husband quickly so I wouldn't be an old widow left alone like Naomi. Still others told me I was crazy for taking care of someone with whom I had no blood relationship. I knew to place that kind of advice in its *proper place. It just wasn't for me, and it didn't fit my story. Those people may have had good intentions, but their advice was not what I followed.*

However, when Naomi told me to go see Boaz one night, I knew I could trust her advice. Naomi had a stake in this game, too. I was taking care of Naomi, and Boaz was making sure we had enough grain to eat. I knew Naomi could be hurt if I made the wrong move, just as I could be hurt. She was now my partner and collaborator. I could trust her. We both had a destiny to win or lose.

B e careful whose advice you take. Not all advice is offered with the right motives. And although you can't shut off all advice, it is wise to be discerning and to do your due diligence when accepting advice. Consider what the advice giver has to lose or gain from your failing or succeeding. Check out the fruit he or she bears; is it the type of fruit you want to grow or would you rather leave it on the ground? Advice can be valuable along this road to your destiny— but be aware and alert.

Giver of Wisdom: I need your discernment when taking advice from others. Help me know what to follow and what to release.

◇◇

Ruth's Destiny Steps

Reach out to a mentor today.

Take a Destiny follower out to lunch. Share a cup of coffee. Figure out if you can help them as they help you broaden your view and continue in your creative zone.

Look for an opportunity to learn from a person younger than you.

Break out of an old pattern; try something new.

Envision the rest of your life as a canvas. What will you draw today that will leave a legacy tomorrow?

◇◇

Bathsheba's Story

2 Samuel 11:2-27 (NLT)

Late one afternoon, after his midday rest, David got out of bed and was walking on the roof of the palace. As he looked out over the city, he noticed a woman of unusual beauty taking a bath. He sent someone to find out who she was, and he was told, "She is Bathsheba, the daughter of Eliam and the wife of Uriah the Hittite." Then David sent messengers to get her; and when she came to the palace, he slept with her. She had just completed the purification rites after having her menstrual period. Then she returned home. Later, when Bathsheba discovered that she was pregnant, she sent David a message, saying, "I'm pregnant."

Then David sent word to Joab: "Send me Uriah the Hittite." So Joab sent him to David. When Uriah arrived, David asked him how Joab and the army were getting along and how the war was progressing. Then he told Uriah, "Go on home and relax." David even sent a gift to Uriah after he had left the palace. But Uriah didn't go home. He slept that night at the palace entrance with the king's palace guard.

When David heard that Uriah had not gone home, he summoned him and asked, "What's the matter? Why didn't you go home last night after being away for so long?"

Uriah replied, "The Ark and the armies of Israel and Judah are living in tents, and Joab and my master's men are camping in the open fields. How could I go home to wine and dine and sleep with my wife? I swear that I would never do such a thing."

"Well, stay here today," David told him, "and tomorrow you may return to the army." So Uriah stayed in Jerusalem that day and the next. Then David invited him to dinner and got him drunk. But even then he couldn't get Uriah to go home to his wife. Again he slept at the palace entrance with the king's palace guard.

So the next morning David wrote a letter to Joab and gave it to Uriah to deliver. The letter instructed Joab, "Station Uriah on the front lines where the battle is fiercest. Then pull back so that he will be killed." So Joab assigned Uriah to a spot close to the city wall where he knew the enemy's strongest men were fighting. And when the enemy soldiers came out of the city to fight, Uriah the Hittite was killed along with several other Israelite soldiers.

Then Joab sent a battle report to David. He told his

messenger, "Report all the news of the battle to the king. But he might get angry and ask, 'Why did the troops go so close to the city? Didn't they know there would be shooting from the walls? Wasn't Abimelech son of Gideon killed at Thebez by a woman who threw a millstone down on him from the wall? Why would you get so close to the wall?' Then tell him, 'Uriah the Hittite was killed, too.'"

So the messenger went to Jerusalem and gave a complete report to David. "The enemy came out against us in the open fields," he said. "And as we chased them back to the city gate, the archers on the wall shot arrows at us. Some of the king's men were killed, including Uriah the Hittite."

"Well, tell Joab not to be discouraged," David said. "The sword devours this one today and that one tomorrow! Fight harder next time, and conquer the city!"

When Uriah's wife heard that her husband was dead, she mourned for him. When the period of mourning was over, David sent for her and brought her to the palace, and she became one of his wives. Then she gave birth to a son. But the LORD was displeased with what David had done.

2 Samuel 12:24-25 (NLT)

Then David comforted Bathsheba, his wife, and slept with her. She became pregnant and gave birth to a son, and David named him Solomon. The LORD loved the child and sent word through Nathan the prophet that they should name him Jedidiah (which means "beloved of the LORD"), as the LORD had commanded.

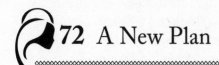

72 A New Plan

Then David comforted his wife Bathsheba, and he went to her and made love to her. She gave birth to a son, and they named him Solomon. The LORD loved him.

2 Samuel 12:24 (NIV)

My life spiraled out of control quickly. My best laid plans seemed to blow up in my face. In a matter of about nine months, my life went from great to pretty much horrific. I was married to a strong and valiant man, a proud soldier. When he was sent off to war, I somehow got caught up in a serious scandal. If you don't know about it, check out the story in 2 Samuel 12.

Basically, my happy home was torn apart. I was forced to sleep with the king—even though I was married. And I got pregnant. I was hurt and ashamed. When I told the king that I was pregnant, he wanted me to sleep with my husband so that my husband would think that the baby was his; well, that didn't work. My husband was such a good man and faithful soldier that he wouldn't indulge in sex while his men were still fighting. He didn't sleep with me, so I couldn't say the baby was his.

When the king found out, he sent my husband back to war with orders to have him killed (well, murdered). I was then taken as the king's wife. Then even more tragedy struck. The baby I was carrying died right after birth. Talk about crushing. The one innocent thing still left in my life was now dead. My hope withered. The pieces of my broken world continued to crumple.

I was tempted to mourn endlessly. I had lost a life that I carefully carried inside of me for nine months, and I had lost my first husband to a terrible tragedy that I couldn't even talk about. The pain seemed unbearable. My days and nights were filled with darkness. It didn't seem like this storm would ever clear up. My light of day seemed far, far away.

But God eventually replaced my ashes with beauty. While I wouldn't wish my story on my worst enemy—my pain was real—my story doesn't end in pain. Even though my journey with my husband and newborn baby was cut short by the sins of oth-

ers, new life was still in me. I gave birth to another
son—Solomon, who became a wise king and a part
of the lineage of Christ. I was charged with rais-
ing him and showing him character and strength.
Our household was tumultuous at times; but as his
mother, I did my best to instill good values in Solo-
mon. I had a new job to do. I had a new path in life
to take. I had new meaning.

When your life throws you a curve ball or takes a drastic detour, it can be tempting to throw in the towel and forget about all the great ideas you may have had planted inside of you. Instead of finding the strength to go on, you want to wither up and die.

When tragedy strikes, mourn, cry, and pray. Seek God's strength for healing—and when it is time, get up, and move on the new path. Life doesn't end when a path is blocked or cut off. Trust God to fill your void when things don't go your way. Lean and depend on God to give you a new vision toward your destiny. God has created each of us with a purpose and a destiny. Don't let any detour stop you; there is another way and another path.

Healer and Helper God: I come to you as an empty vessel. I feel torn and broken. I need you to fill me up and show me a new path. I need you now.

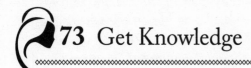

73 Get Knowledge

Give instruction to the wise, and they will become wiser still; teach the righteous and they will gain in learning.

Proverbs 9:9 (NRSV)

Many people just know me as Bathsheba, the married woman King David saw bathing. After he slept with me, tried to trick my husband, had my husband killed, and took me as his wife, we lost our child (2 Samuel 11–12). But there is more to my story, much more to how I lived out my destiny.

Later in life, when King David was near death, I saved the kingdom. I got some knowledge from a very trusted source, the prophet Nathan. He said that another man was taking over David's kingdom even though David had promised that my son, Solomon, would be his successor (1 Kings 1:11-17). But Nathan had a plan for us to right this wrong.

Because I knew Nathan was a man of God who brought truth to situations, I trusted his knowledge. I knew him to be a wise man, and I followed his advice. I didn't bury my head in the sand and wish the problem away. I acted upon the knowledge I received and boldly stepped to the king on his dying bed. Even though I was one of David's wives, it was still dangerous for a queen to request a meeting with the king. But my actions were prompted by the knowledge I received from a trusted source. To fully reach my destiny, I had to put my knowledge into action and help get Solomon on the throne before it was too late.

Following my destiny took courage and strength and the wisdom to listen to the right advice.

A Destiny follower knows when to listen to wisdom. In fact, those living out their destiny know the importance of seeking knowledge and wisdom, and acting on what they know—even in tumultuous times. The road toward Destiny will involve intentionally gaining knowledge and purposefully pursuing wisdom. You don't have to know everything, but you do need to know who you can trust for information in areas that you are not familiar with—or not fully knowledgeable. And you will need to be a person who pursues knowledge and wisdom. When you know better, you will do better—and a Destiny follower always wants to improve and do more and do better.

Your advisors will be able to help you; know their areas of strength and rely on them. Your mentors should have a proven track record in some of the areas you are trying to get to. Surround yourself with people who are constantly learning and evolving on their route to Destiny. When you are in the company of these types of people, you can trust their information and be better prepared to act upon your own destiny. You, too, will be encouraged to increase your knowledge and not to limit yourself. Your willingness to move into the vistas of greater knowledge is an important quality that will invite Destiny to open her doors to you.

Wise and All-Knowing God: I promise to be a lifelong learner on my road toward Destiny. I will seek your wisdom in all things I do and surround myself with trustworthy advisors. I am ready to move forward. Amen.

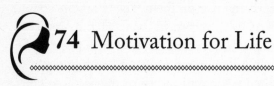# 74 Motivation for Life

Sing praises to the LORD, O you his faithful ones, and give thanks to his holy name. For his anger is but for a moment; his favor is for a lifetime. Weeping may linger for the night, but joy comes with the morning.

Psalm 30:4-5 (NRSV)

When you read about my life, you see struggle and death and blood and defeat. It's all there. But that's not all to my story; many have wondered how I was able to live a fulfilled and contented life in the midst of the ugly things that happened.

I shed a lot of tears in this life—when I was taken by the great King David, when my husband was murdered, when my baby died, when the people whispered about me. But I couldn't sit around idly crying about all that happened to me. I refused to live this life as a victim. I knew I was called to more, and I had to press through all of the ugly to get to my purpose.

I am in the lineage of Jesus. I played a role in bringing forth an eternal promise that would change the world. I found contentment in knowing that I was doing what would fulfill God's promise. Although life threw me many curve balls, I was motivated to keep going. I was motivated to pursue my purpose and destiny despite the struggles. I saw the big picture and knew that somehow I was a part of the salvation story, and I had to live to bring it about. I focused on the purpose, not the pain. That's how I was able to live in the midst of the struggle.

I n my book *Destiny*, I talk about famous people who withstood major struggles and still lived contented lives. Coretta Scott King, the widow of Civil Rights Drum Major, Dr. Martin Luther King, Jr., told me herself that she was destined to be the support system to this great icon. She was called to live the life she did, raise her children, and help him bring about the changes he did. That was her destiny. And even though his death came early and she was left to raise children alone, she didn't get caught up in the pain and struggle. She was able to be content because she accepted her role in destiny and lived it to her fullest ability.

I also wrote briefly about Nelson Mandela, the civil rights leader in South Africa who spent more than twenty-seven years in prison because of his fight for everyone's rights. When he was released from prison, he was able to rise to the highest office in South Africa. If he had focused on the pain and struggles he had to endure while fighting, surely he wouldn't have been able to forgive and become a beacon of light for reconciliation in that country and an example for the world. He found contentment in knowing he was living out his purpose. He was putting his skills into action to fulfill his destiny. Was twenty-seven years of imprisonment, separated from his family, painful? Of course it was. But he found contentment in his purpose, not in his pain.

We'd be wise to use Mrs. King, Mr. Mandela, and Bathsheba as examples of how we can live through pain and stay motivated to find contentment in a life of struggle as we press toward our purpose.

God, My Sustainer: I praise you for taking care of me through life's ups and downs. I thank you for being with me on the mountain tops, in the valleys, and in every place in between. You are amazing and awesome.

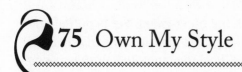# 75 Own My Style

For it was you who formed my inward parts; you knit me together in my mother's womb. I praise you, for I am fearfully and wonderfully made. Wonderful are your works; that I know very well.

Psalm 139:13-14 (NRSV)

When I first became David's wife, I held onto a lot of shame. My entrance into the queen's palace was not a story I would brag about. For a while, I buried my head and didn't really feel like a queen or like I could rightfully claim a place in the palace.

David's other wives were so different. I saw them as strong and beautiful and more "legal" than I was. Michal and Maacah were daughters of kings who were given to David. They were already royalty so I'm sure they knew the ropes. Abigail, heralded as a wise, smart queen, became his wife after her husband died—not because David had him murdered.

The other wives seemed to fit in. And then, there was me—the woman people talked about, the one known for taking a bath and tempting the king, the one whose child had died.

As I observed the other wives, the beautiful and smart queens, I began to pick up some things. I saw how they talked, how they took care of things, and who they were. I saw them walk as queens and live as if they belonged right there in the palace. Eventually—after much prayer and contemplation—I, too, began to see myself as a queen.

I learned to hold my head up high and take care of my business. I realized I had a destiny. I recognized I had authentic gifts. I learned that God created me—just like God created the others. I was made well. I was made awesomely and distinctly. I, too, had something to contribute. I, too, had a purpose and could live out my destiny. I learned to be grateful for the example set forth by the other queens— and find my own unique style and walk in it.

Observing others can help us set the bar of excellence high for ourselves. But at some point, there must be a breaking point—where one respects, admires, and learns from others but then turns inward to connect to his or her authentic expression of talent. You have to know for yourself that you have been created with gifts and skills and made for a purpose. You have to know your authentic self and what you can do—and own it. Walk in it. No one wants a replica. We hardly believe copy cats. Each person is created to be authentic so use your own style to meet your destiny.

When you know who you are in God, you can be happy for the success of someone else. That person doesn't intimidate you—no matter how gifted they are or how many accolades they receive. You know who you are and what you are good at—and you can celebrate yourself while celebrating others. You are grateful to have examples to gain information from; but you also know that there's a point where you break free from following others and live your life in your own style and with your own purpose.

Masterful Architect: I claim the truth that I am fearfully and wonderfully made. I thank you for creating me just as you saw fit. Help me to walk in my own style as I live out my purpose.

76 Honor the Process

There's more to come: We continue to shout our praise even when we're hemmed in with troubles, because we know how troubles can develop passionate patience in us, and how that patience in turn forges the tempered steel of virtue, keeping us alert for whatever God will do next. In alert expectancy such as this, we're never left feeling shortchanged. Quite the contrary—we can't round up enough containers to hold everything God generously pours into our lives through the Holy Spirit!

Romans 5:3-5 (MSG)

Looking back over my life, I sometimes wonder if it would have been easier to live it backwards; you know, to see the ending first. That way I would have been able to see how God was piecing together what I needed to reach my destiny. But unfortunately, that's not how life works. To reach my destiny, I had to trust the process and take it step by step.

When my life took that drastic turn and I lost my first husband, I was confused and saddened. How could life take such a sharp turn so quickly? Then when I married David and gave birth to our child, the baby died shortly after he was born. I didn't know what to do. I was grief-stricken again, just a few months after my life had already begun to unravel.

In all of that sadness, my destiny was still being revealed. My purpose and destiny were still awaiting my arrival—even though I felt horrible, even though I had experienced the worst type of tragedies. In those years as King David's wife, I gained a lot of character and fortitude and faith—things I didn't have before.

I noticed that I grew patient. I grew bolder. I grew nurturing. I learned that God can turn sorrow into joy. And I learned to trust God no matter what. Then one day, I realized that I had gained enough courage and fortitude to secure my son Solomon's place on the throne—even though he wasn't the oldest son. As I look back over my life, each phase, I see I was still able to meet my destiny—by taking it one step at a time and learning what I needed to know.

Steps are a part of our maturation. If we get what God has in store for us too soon, we just might mess it up. Not many people appreciate steps. We want to skip a few and get to the top—the place we desire to be. But steps serve a purpose. Steps are a part of the process. Steps teach us how to get to new levels—deliberately, if slowly. Think about what you learned along the journey and how it has gotten you to this point in life. Now imagine having skipped some of those steps.

When you consider the steps toward Destiny, you realize that there really are no short cuts. You can't take the elevator straight to the top. You will need each part of the process to complete the picture and learn what is needed—patience, virtue, skills, perseverance, reliance on God, and so much more. Take each step with patience, soaking up all God has instilled in and around you with gratitude.

Eternal and Everlasting God: Thank you for each step of the process on my road toward Destiny. Give me an attitude of gratitude as I take one more step this day.

77 Engage Simultaneously

Wise men and women are always learning, always listening for fresh insights. A gift gets attention; it buys the attention of eminent people.

Proverbs 18:15-16 (MSG)

I realized that I was engaged in my destiny when I stopped trying to make things fit perfectly into my world. I learned to engage my passion and interests and soon realized that new opportunities were open and available to me. There was a time when I sat and wondered why I wasn't fulfilled and why my life didn't turn out like I had thought it would. But I let go of those thoughts and began to learn from life. I learned from everything—people, stories, events. I listened and I observed. I thought new thoughts and experienced new things.

Soon I learned that I really loved doing some

things. In fact, I learned that I was pretty good at some things, too. As I learned more about my gifts and skills and talents, I saw more ways to use them. By opening my eyes and becoming exposed, I opened the door to follow the path of my destiny and to live a fulfilled life.

It's wonderful that our post-industrial nation has grown to allow us to gain exposure through more than one career. A couple of generations ago, a person who had several careers often was perceived as immature or unstable. Back then, a person found a job or established a business and did only that for a lifetime. Now we think in terms of multiple streams of income—making money from various fields of endeavor.

How do we decide to do this? Exposure. You may work as an accountant for a small corporation. Then, to express your creative side, you might have a small business as a wedding coordinator. You may also blog about dating and relationships. Exposure teaches you that you have multiple talents and can engage in many endeavors, even simultaneously.

The path of life and the path toward Destiny can be filled with many twists and turns. There really is no straight line from point A to Z in Destiny. Your path toward Destiny is not locked into one position, one time, or even one career choice. It's not too late to do what you love—whether that is in a full-time position, as a volunteer, or on the side.

Sometimes our 9-to-5 jobs pay the bills so we can enjoy our passions on the side. Other times we discover our passions while working, which can make room for our gifts to grow and blossom and create new opportunities that we had never considered. Exposure helps you open your eyes so doors can be opened.

Creator and Sustainer: I am grateful that you have created me with passions and interests. Remind me to be open to seeing new opportunities in new places and in new ways. I look forward to walking the path toward my destiny.

78 Exposure's Price

"Be strong. Take courage. Don't be intimidated. Don't give them a second thought because GOD, your God, is striding ahead of you. [God is] right there with you. [God] won't let you down; [God] won't leave you."

Deuteronomy 31:6 (MSG)

Because of the shameful, hurtful, and tragic way I became David's wife, I often felt insecure. I wasn't royalty. I wasn't given to the king by my daddy. I was the side piece (2 Samuel 11:2-4). I spent a long time grappling with my inadequacy. But eventually, I decided to trust God's hand in this whole scenario. While God didn't ordain David's sin, I knew God could use our broken pieces and turn them into something beautiful. So, even when my life took a downward spiral, God amazingly brought about redemption.

When I truly began to believe God had a plan for my life, I was able to walk in that path. I figured I was in this place in life and I needed to put aside the shame of how I got here—and live it. If God was with me when all the tragic stuff was happening, surely God was still with me. I had been exposed to all I had seen for a reason, and I wasn't going to let shame stop me from following my destiny. I had wasted enough time. I had a destiny to meet.

Choosing to be open to exposure will require that you look at things differently and pay attention to life again. Engage. Read. Give. Pray. Act. Sacrifice. Think. Plan. Strategize. Assess. New experiences, new knowledge, and new environments can completely change your approach to life.

Fear. Excitement. Anxiety. Nervousness. Restlessness. Insecurity. These feelings are the price of exposure. Whether you click with your new environment or not, your exposure to it is always a blessing. The fact that God has exposed you to something is always a sign that it can be yours. God is exposing you so you can absorb Destiny in the deepest part of your soul. Breathe in and believe, and let God open the doors to Destiny through exposure.

Heavenly Lord: Help me to set aside anxiety, fear, and insecurity when I am exposed to new things, people, and places. I know you are with me and will never leave me.

79 Don't Major in Minors

≈≈

The Master said, "Martha, dear Martha, you're fussing far too much and getting yourself worked up over nothing. One thing only is essential, and Mary has chosen it—it's the main course, and won't be taken from her."

Luke 10:41-42 (MSG)

Living as one of the king's wives in a kingdom filled with David's wives was not always easy. Many might wonder how I even endured. How did I get to my destiny, groom Solomon for his place on the throne and take care of my other business. It was not easy, but I did learn something very important. I learned to focus on the main things in life.

It was sometimes tempting to bicker and fight about small things; you know, the little things in a day that go wrong. We can be so easily swayed to respond to everything—the mean look, the nega-

tive tone, the lies. People whispered about me. But I learned to focus on what my goals in this life truly were. I wanted to meet my destiny. I wanted to take care of my family. I wanted to bring honor to the throne. My position as a king's wife and later as Queen Mother could be used for good if I stayed focused.

Meditating on God's Word and promises can help you stay focused on your goals and to keep the main thing the main thing. Don't give in to the temptations of pettiness. Rise above it and keep your mind focused. The Scripture in today's passage reminds us of the importance of maintaining focus on our purpose—our main goals in life. One of those goals is to stay in tune and connected with God. That, after all, is how we stay connected to our purpose and can meet our destiny. Quiet time, reflecting on the teachings of Christ, worship, singing, and praying are all ways we can choose the main thing.

We can also remember to let little things pass us by or relegate minor issues to others to handle or fix. If we expend all of our energy fixing small things, responding to every issue, we will not have the energy to truly fulfill our purpose and meet up with Destiny. You've got to learn to conserve that energy and stay focused on the main thing.

Smart managers—of fortune 500 companies, homes, and organizations—know that they cannot do everything. They are in tune with their gifting and spend most of their energy in that arena. If they have to fix every broken issue themselves, they are shortchanging their gifts and their ability to fully use them. They hire capable people to handle issues that they don't need to handle. Again they know how to keep the main thing their main thing.

Keep focused on God and learn to leave the small, minor issues alone. Make the main thing your main thing.

My Prince of Peace: Center me each moment so I may keep my focus on you and your amazing plans for my life. When I am tempted to get flustered over minor issues, refocus my attention on the main purpose.

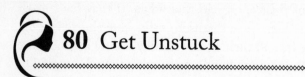

80 Get Unstuck

Then you will understand what is right and good, and right from wrong, and you will know what you should do. For wisdom will come into your heart. And much learning will be pleasing to your soul. Good thinking will keep you safe. Understanding will watch over you.

Proverbs 2:9-11 (NLV)

I didn't stop dreaming or trying to reach my own destiny just because I was King David's wife. After the pain of losing my first husband and my little baby lessened—it really never fully went away; it just lessened—I accepted my place as one of David's queens. But I couldn't give into the temptation to just be a queen, happy to be in a great man's life. I needed to keep pursuing my purpose. I needed to fulfill a destiny of my own.

I began to assess my life and asked what I needed

to change and how. I was honest and shared what I liked about my life, myself, and my skills. I learned what I didn't know, and I shook off some of the negative things I thought about myself—and the things that others said about me. I couldn't do anything about the past, but I could use my current position to get me to the next level and to my destiny. I learned to be wise and discerning.

Life isn't always going to go your way, but you don't have to let what happens to you bury you or cause you to give up on your own dream. Use what is there to step forward. Throw away what is hindering you so you can be free to run this race well.

Getting unstuck is not always easy—even when you are determined to meet your destiny. Think about where you are in life now and what may be holding you back. Not everything will need to be fixed or released. Discernment teaches you what to work on and what to build on. It's important to know the difference. You should know what is an asset and what is a liability. Use the assets to get to your destiny and change the liabilities, one by one. But don't become overwhelmed with the negative stuff. Whatever you have going on in your life right now shouldn't bury you; use it as a stepping stone to get to the next level. See the good so you can be encouraged and motivated to keep stepping higher and going further.

I tell a story in *Destiny* about a farmer whose donkey fell in a well. After several failed attempts to rescue the donkey, the farmer's friends convinced him it would be better to bury the donkey alive rather than hurting him further by trying to pull him out of the well. So eventually, the farmer started pouring dirt into the well to cover the hole, but the donkey was very much alive. He refused to be buried by the dirt that kept coming down the hole. He shook each shovel-full off of his back, causing the dirt to drop to the ground. It soon hardened, and he was able to step on the dirt.

As each pile of dirt streamed down, it became a mound for the donkey to stand on. When the owner decided to take one last look down the well to say good-bye to the donkey, imagine his surprise when he saw the donkey rising to the top because he was standing on all of that dirt.

You can use life's issues the same way: shake the dirt off of your back and stand on what's left. Use each opportunity—good, bad, indifferent—to reach another level and a step closer to your destiny.

❖　❖　❖　❖

My Rock, My Salvation: I will build upon all you have given me so that I may reach my destiny. I will not let dirt bury me, but instead I will keep growing and moving closer to you and closer to my destiny.

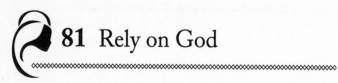

81 Rely on God

xxxxxxxxxxxxxxxxxxxxxxxxxxxxxxxxxxxxxxxxxxxxxxxxxxxxxxxxxxxxxxxxxxxxxxx

For I can do everything through Christ, who gives me strength.

Philippians 4:13 (NLT)

King David responded, "Call Bathsheba!" So she came back in and stood before the king. And the king repeated his vow: "As surely as the LORD lives, who has rescued me from every danger, your son Solomon will be the next king and will sit on my throne this very day, just as I vowed to you before the LORD, the God of Israel." Then Bathsheba bowed down with her face to the ground before the king and exclaimed, "May my lord King David live forever!"

1 Kings 1:28-31 (NLT)

My son Solomon almost didn't get the throne David had promised to him and to me. David was old, sickly, and nearing death. Even as one of his wives, I didn't get to see him much; it's the way things worked. But the prophet Nathan told me about an attempt to take the throne from David's successor, *my son Solomon, and Nathan wanted me to alert a dying David of this controversy. Nathan made a request of me that required me to go into David's chambers and ask him a question.*

By this time in my life, I was not used to asking for much. I was a queen and was soon to be Queen Mother—so I thought. I didn't want to bow down to David and make a request. I thought my days of living like David's subject had come to an end. But deep down I knew going in and requesting one more thing from David was the right thing to do for my destiny and for my son's destiny.

In this situation, my true strength became my ability to discern the moment and the situation. I decided it was wiser to bow down to the old king now than to have my son's throne lost forever. It was a promise from God and from David to have Solomon on the throne, so I did what I needed to do.

There is an old saying: "There's a time and a place for everything." And I would add to that saying: "And you've got to know what time it is and what place you are in." In other words, you've got to know when to use your strength and when to rely on God's strength, when to move and when to sit still.

Strength can be a tricky thing. Many people I know have no problem standing up for themselves and being assertive. Often times they want to push ahead and make things happen—because they know they can. These are not the people lacking self-confidence and assertiveness. These are my warriors, the people who are used to getting it done. But even the warrior spirit needs to be discerning because strength used in the wrong place can be a weakness—which can also make the road toward destiny seem distant and illusive.

However, when strength (or any gift) is used in the right place and used in the proper perspective, it is positive. When the warrior spirit hooks up with God's strength and relies on God to know when and how to move, watch out. Finding the balance of doing all you can and relying on God to do the rest takes faith and practice. Stay in tune with God and know that you have a role to play; but so does God. Let God's strength carry you. Let God's strength do the impossible in you.

Powerful and Almighty God: Give me wisdom to rely on your strength. Give me discernment to know how to use my strength and when to watch you work.

82 Listen to the Counsel

✕✕

Then Nathan said to Bathsheba, Solomon's mother, "Have you not heard that Adonijah son of Haggith has become king and our lord David does not know it? Now therefore come, let me give you advice, so that you may save your own life and the life of your son Solomon.

1 Kings 1:11-12 (NRSV)

It's better to be wise than strong; intelligence outranks muscle any day. Strategic planning is the key to warfare; to win, you need a lot of good counsel.

Proverbs 24:5-6 (MSG)

By the time King David was about to die, I had grown tremendously and was enjoying the journey toward my destiny. I was living what I thought was my destiny. I had worked hard to prepare Solomon for the kingship, and I thought we had it secured. All we needed to do was to keep living and the things *promised would come to pass.*

Nathan had served in the role of prophet and mentor to David for many years, and Nathan had always looked out for David—even when he had to give him hard news and difficult advice (see 2 Samuel 12:1-15). So when Nathan alerted me to an issue that threatened Solomon's destiny—and mine—I listened. I did what he said and success was ours.

How do you know whether you need a mentor? When all that is within you hasn't produced the expected outcomes, you need to enhance *what* you know with *whom* you know. There's someone who's been where you are and can help you step forward. God often answers prayer *with* people rather than *for* them. Many times the solutions you seek are often provided by the people with whom you have relationships. Such connections will be your greatest resource; so protect them at all cost. These associations are more than simply mentors to mentees. They often are the critical conduits that empower you to be in the right frame of mind and the right setting to evolve to your next level.

You can't reach new vistas without expanding your circle with new affiliations. The newness can be scary, yet at the same time exhilarating! A life that lacks spontaneity and adventure has become predictable. If your life can be defined as a droll existence void of destiny, then it's time to take a step! Listen to trusted people and move forward.

God, My Constant Companion: Lead me and guide me to the right people and relationships that will help me move forward toward my destiny. I am grateful for the connections you are bringing my way.

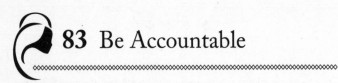

83 Be Accountable

Take good counsel and accept correction—that's the way to live wisely and well.

Proverbs 19:20 (MSG)

I can tell you a lot about my relationship with Nathan; he was a true mentor and advisor to both David and me. And it really started off with pure trust. David trusted Nathan to tell him the truth, no matter what. It was Nathan who confronted David about me and my husband (2 Samuel 12:1-10). Wise Nathan told David a story about a poor man and a rich man. The rich man killed the poor man's one and only animal to serve the rich man's guest instead of using an animal from his own large flock. David was outraged by this story but soon became repentant when Nathan told him that the story was really what David had done to Uriah, my husband.

David, a rich man, had taken me from the noble Uriah. Nathan helped David confess to God and repent from his sin (Psalm 51). Nathan was a trusted advisor.

I, likewise, learned to trust Nathan, too. And I could tell him anything—the good, bad, and ugly parts of life. I'm glad I listened to Nathan. I'm thankful for good counsel.

In order for a mentor to help you, you're going to have to be honest and vulnerable. You're going to have to admit what you don't know, share what you are afraid of, and be up front. It's not easy to admit some of those things to ourselves, let alone to a mentor. But if you want to reach your destiny, it will be important to have people to whom you are accountable—people that you trust to tell you what you need to hear, not just what you want to hear. It's a wise way to live. It's the only way to live if you want to reach your destiny and be fulfilled.

To gain the most out of your mentor-mentee relationship, you should recognize that someone that you will not be accountable to cannot mentor you. Imagine the impossibility of a mentor relationship with someone with whom you will not share the full realities of your struggles and success. That would be a frustrating experience for both the mentor and the mentee. Accountability requires transparency; therefore, you have to establish a level of trust with your mentor that will allow you the vulnerability of exposing your deficiencies and insecurities. Most people wear their accomplishments as a camouflage to hide their inadequacies.

Mentors get to look behind the façade to help you fill in the blanks that are masked from public view. They need to know your emotions. They need access to information about the areas at home that are in crisis because of your accomplishments. If you keep up a wall with your mentor, he or she will never be able to penetrate your mind to address the real challenges you face. You will probably gain a few helpful tips, but you won't reap the full benefit of someone walking alongside you on your Destiny journey.

Most of us can excel in one or two areas of life with little assistance. Mentors will help you develop a 360° range of success. That doesn't mean every area of your life will run smoothly at all times. Most of us are dealing with some level of trouble or challenge at any point in our lives. We all need someone that we trust to serve as a check and balance to help us live the full life we desire. Mentors ask you the hard questions. When you're soaring high from career advancement, your mentor will inquire about your marriage. You've got lots of money in the bank, but your mentor will ask how you're inspiring your kids to have their own goals and dreams apart from your accomplishments.

Make sure your mentor is one to whom you can be accountable. Be open and honest to get the most out of your relationship and to push you toward your destiny.

All-Knowing, Wise God: I vow to be vulnerable with you, myself, and my trusted mentors. I want to live a fulfilled and balanced life. I know I need help keeping all things in perspective as I journey toward my destiny. I thank you for your provision through my mentors.

 **84** Guard My Heart

〰〰〰〰〰〰〰〰〰〰〰〰〰〰〰〰〰〰〰〰〰〰〰〰〰〰〰

Keep vigilant watch over your heart; that's where life starts. Don't talk out of both sides of your mouth; avoid careless banter, white lies, and gossip. Keep your eyes straight ahead; ignore all sideshow distractions. Watch your step, and the road will stretch out smooth before you. Look neither right nor left; leave evil in the dust.

Proverbs 4:23-27 (MSG)

Living in the king's palace among many people was not always easy, and I had to learn to guard my heart to stay on my path toward the destiny that God was calling me to walk in. I could have gotten caught up in all that David was doing and all that God had called him to be, but that would not have helped me. David had his own path. David had his own directions and instructions from God. I had to find my path and I had to find my destiny.

David is celebrated throughout the Bible and his-

tory, but that was his destiny. I needed to do my part and contribute to God's kingdom. When I learned to focus on what God was telling me, Bathsheba, to do, I could better understand that I had a special calling as well. I had to play my role in the script of life—and in time, I did. I learned to follow God and do what God told me to do. I learned to focus on my part and to live.

Passion takes energy. Vision takes energy. Strategy takes energy. As Destiny draws you, you will need to invest yourself there, which means you don't have time for energy-draining attitudes, feelings, and emotions—like being jealous, intimidated, or scared. You have been chosen to play the role that is your destiny. You have a calling.

Simply do what you do. No person was meant to be someone else. Every person's destiny offers fulfillment in doing what God has destined that person to do. Find your purpose, the calling for your unique gifts. Enjoy *your* life. Keep your heart tuned to God and the things God has called *you* to do. Don't focus on others; you need that energy to walk your own path.

Amazing and Awesome Creator: Guide me on the path

you have designed just for me. Help me not to focus on others but to focus on you and what you are calling me to do.

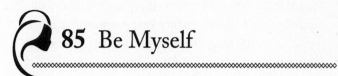

85 Be Myself

Since this is the kind of life we have chosen, the life of the Spirit,
let us make sure that we do not just hold it as an idea in our heads
or a sentiment in our hearts, but work out its implications in every
detail of our lives. That means we will not compare ourselves with
each other as if one of us were better and another worse. We have
far more interesting things to do with our lives. Each of us is an
original.

Galatians 5:25-26 (MSG)

I didn't always see clearly how God was bringing
about my destiny. For a while I was stuck in David's
shadow and I was miserable. I had endured the loss
of my first husband and the loss of my baby and
was now living in a new world and a new place. I
sometimes wondered if I'd ever find my destiny or if I
was destined to be just another woman in a crowd.

I foolishly looked at others and wanted to do what they did.

I tried on several roles before I found my path. It took a long time, but I eventually understood from God that part of my destiny was preparing a place for Solomon as king. He needed care and he needed instruction. In order for me to train up this king, I needed to be okay with myself. I needed to work on my issues so I wouldn't impart them to my child. I stopped looking at others and their successes, and I focused on my path and becoming my best self. It was a process, but God helped me get there.

Everyone has a path and a process to go through. Be you and let God direct your path. Frustration with Destiny's process can cause us to become envious of people who seem to have already arrived. Remember they, too, endured a process. Every success has a back story that you cannot see.

I am not accountable for the gifts God gave someone else. God does not expect me to produce beyond the level of gifts given me. My only obligation is to use the gifts God has given me to the best of my ability.

The gifts God gave you are not the same as the gifts he has given anyone else. So why look at what God has done in someone else's life? If you compare yourself with others, you'll never be at peace. Celebrate the skin you're in and be happy pursuing your own destiny.

Divine Destiny Giver: Thank you for creating me as you have created me. I desire to walk in the unique gifting and purpose you've designed for me. Help me to be the best person you have created me to be and not to focus on or compare myself to anyone else.

86 Press Forward

〰〰〰〰〰〰〰〰〰〰〰〰〰〰〰〰〰〰〰〰〰〰〰〰〰〰〰〰〰

I don't mean to say that I have already achieved these things or that I have already reached perfection. But I press on to possess that perfection for which Christ Jesus first possessed me. No, dear brothers and sisters, I have not achieved it, but I focus on this one thing: Forgetting the past and looking forward to what lies ahead, I press on to reach the end of the race and receive the heavenly prize for which God, through Christ Jesus, is calling us.

Philippians 3:12-14 (NLT)

I had to learn to let the past be the past and keep growing and expecting new meaning in my new place. I knew I was in a new place for a new reason, but it wasn't always easy. When things were going well, I rarely thought about my old life. But when things got crazy—and they often did in King David's home—I thought about how life would have been or could have been if this didn't happen, if my husband wasn't killed, if I hadn't . . . . I soon learned that this type of thinking was not helpful in looking forward and going forward to meet my destiny. I had to keep pressing my way toward the path and plans God had for me. It's how I got through the tough days.

When you arrive in a new place on the journey toward your destiny, it is very tempting to look back and long for the old place and the old days, especially when things get tough in the new arena. The key to completing your journey to Destiny is to resist the urge to retreat into the familiar spaces of the past. In a new space, yesterday can look pretty good because it's familiar. But if you could go back to yesterday, it would not be as warm, wonderful, and inviting as you think. Ignore the tendency to glamorize what you left behind. If the place you left had been all that great, you wouldn't have moved out of it to answer Destiny's call.

Not yet arriving at your destination can cause you to glamorize even an unhappy past and prompt you to doubt where you are headed. You begin to wonder if you really have what it takes. Put that to rest right now. You have everything you need at the time you need it. Where you were does not indicate where you are going. You had what you needed for then, and you have what you need now. You gained the lessons you needed from where you were then. Now it's time to move on.

Let go what was in your past and let it stay there. Be thankful for the memories. Be grateful for the lessons learned, even the hard ones. Feel relief that the bad experiences are over and that you survived them. Keep moving because you can't walk forward while looking back.

There is so much more of life for Destiny to unfold to you. Give Destiny a chance. Make room for your present. You need all that energy you devote to glamorizing your past to learn the lessons you need to thrive in your present and excel in your future.

My Rock and My Refuge: Forgive me for focusing on my past. Renew in me a right spirit so I may press forward to move into the place you have called me to.

87 Feelings vs. Actions

※※※※※※※※※※※※※※※※※※※※※※※※※※※※※※※※※※※※

Don't you realize that in a race everyone runs, but only one person gets the prize? So run to win! All athletes are disciplined in their training. They do it to win a prize that will fade away, but we do it for an eternal prize. So I run with purpose in every step. I am not just shadowboxing. I discipline my body like an athlete, training it to do what it should. Otherwise, I fear that after preaching to others I myself might be disqualified.

1 Corinthians 9:24-27 (NLT)

Discipline was another lesson I picked up while journeying toward my destiny. I didn't always have it. I didn't know I needed it. I was used to doing things on a whim, when I got the feeling. Living as royalty can spoil you and make you lazy; it's what happens when you are used to getting everything you want or expect to get something just because you want it. But I realized I had a calling and an important job to do. I needed to impart some serious lessons about life to my son, who would one day be king and fulfill an important role. I wanted him to learn about hard work and discipline, too. I didn't want him thinking everything would be easy and handed to him. So I learned to discipline myself. I set a plan in motion and stuck to it, whether I felt like it or not. I learned that I needed to live on purpose to fulfill my purpose, not just live on a whim. I wanted more and I needed discipline to get it.

You may not *feel* like a person of Destiny when you wake up every day, but that's just your feelings. Your *head* will tell you to get up, be on time, and face the daily challenges because Destiny awaits you. Your future is not rooted in how you feel, but in how you act. You cannot base your quest for Destiny on feelings. The way you feel changes based on different variables, but your mind changes based on knowledge and information. Don't give in to your feelings. Emotions are the saboteurs of Destiny. Beat your feelings into captivity through mental discipline.

Discipline says, "I may not like what I have to do today or feel like doing it, but I know what must be done and why I have to do it." Discipline is the domain of the head. Feelings tell you to do what is easy and comfortable, to do what everyone else is doing and satisfy your body. Feelings lead you to make excuses and argue with what your head knows you need to do.

Which one will you go with today? Feelings will fail you. Discipline paves the way toward Destiny.

Amazing Giver of Grace: Give me the discipline to follow my path toward Destiny. Help me to ignore my feelings when they are tempting me.

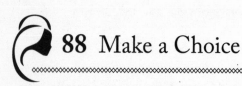 **88** Make a Choice

GOD, *teach me lessons for living so I can stay the course. Give me insight so I can do what you tell me—my whole life one long, obedient response. Guide me down the road of your commandments; I love traveling this freeway! Give me a bent for your words of wisdom, and not for piling up loot. Divert my eyes from toys and trinkets, invigorate me on the pilgrim way. Affirm your promises to me—promises made to all who fear you.*

Psalm 119:33-38 (MSG)

When I moved into King David's palace, I could have settled in and enjoyed the life of being a queen. I could have stayed put right there in the king's quarters, taken care of raising Solomon, and been content. But I knew there was so much more to the world. I didn't necessarily have to move out of the palace to be exposed to it. I just needed to open my mind and be ready for adventures, ready to meet

*different people, and ready to do things most peo-
ple just wouldn't expect a queen to do. I could have
been content, but I chose to be open. I chose to be
alive while living this life.*

*Not everyone affirmed my decision to be a differ-
ent kind of king's wife. Not everyone thought it made
sense for me to engage with people who weren't
royalty. But I hadn't been royalty all of my life, and I
knew there were so many wonderful people to meet
and great places to go—and some lessons to learn
that I couldn't learn from being around people who
were just like me. This exposure made my journey
toward Destiny more enjoyable and more fulfilling.
It informed the way I raised my child, who grew to
be a wise king who carried on the promise of God.*

Exposure is a choice. You don't have to travel half-
way around the world to broaden your exposure. You can broaden yourself by taking a class
or cultivating a new hobby. Exposing yourself to new
knowledge and experiences is a choice that you make,
which causes you not to live in the limited confines that
once nurtured you.

Make a conscious choice to surround yourself with
people who make you want to step up your game, to
learn more, and to do better. Do try to bring along other
willing minds when God blesses you with greater expo-

sure. Share it with people who haven't had the benefit of your experience.

Almighty God: Help me to choose to be exposed to other people, places, and ideas so that I may be invigorated on this Destiny journey.

89 Go with the Flow

xxxxxxxxxxxxxxxxxxxxxxxxxxxxxxxxxxxxxxxxxxxxxxxxxxxxxxxxxxxxxxxxxxxxx

And after you have suffered for a little while, the God of all grace, who has called you to ... eternal glory in Christ, will ... restore, support, strengthen, and establish you.

1 Peter 5:10 (NRSV)

I was determined to walk toward my Destiny, and I had to learn to go with the flow. I didn't learn this overnight nor did it ever become easy. I just felt it was what I needed to do in order to walk the path of Destiny. When my life changed drastically and I faced mourning my husband's death, becoming the king's new wife, and losing our child, I could have just stopped living. I thought about it—more mornings that I care to admit. I felt out of control. But I eventually realized that if I was going to be any good and live the life I was destined to live, I would have to learn how to handle the pain.

I'd have to keep going despite the pain I felt. Some days were harder than others, but kept going. When good came, I rejoiced. When bad came, I remembered how God had brought me through so many other times.

Going with the flow of Destiny doesn't mean you won't experience pain, hurt, anxiety, anger, and loss. It means you don't let it paralyze you and rob you of the opportunity for new life experiences and a new purpose.

When someone is dying after all medical and all resuscitation efforts have failed, there is nothing you can do to stop it. Likewise, you cannot stop the birth of a baby when the water breaks and the mother goes into labor. The only action to take in those birth and death moments is to adapt and adjust to the situation.

No matter how dark it gets, morning comes. Remember to move with the ebb and flow of life if you want to keep going—even when it feels like you should stop. Learn how to move on and find meaningful ways to fill the void the loss created in your life or stretch to accommodate the new member of the family. You don't do so in a day, or because you make a decision. It is a process. But when you keep moving with the flow, you can craft a new way to find meaning in life.

Wonderful and Awesome God: Thank you for reminding me that joy comes in the morning. Help me to keep moving when the darkness feels overwhelming.

90 Comfort to Others

〰〰〰〰〰〰〰〰〰〰〰〰〰〰〰〰〰〰〰〰〰〰〰〰〰〰〰〰〰〰〰〰〰〰〰〰

All praise to God, the Father of our Lord Jesus Christ. God is our merciful Father and the source of all comfort. He comforts us in all our troubles so that we can comfort others. When they are troubled, we will be able to give them the same comfort God has given us.

2 Corinthians 1:3-4 (NLT)

I went through so many tragic events at one time, I wondered if life would ever again make sense. I even questioned whether I had a destiny or not; although I know now that everyone has a destiny. I could not always see it when I was in the midst of pain. But I kept living and kept moving, and eventually saw my purpose. Every detail was not be revealed at once, nor did I even understand what was revealed, but God gave me peace and purpose despite what I'd been through.

After losing my husband and my baby and being forced into a whole new world, I had no idea how God was working or whether I had a destiny. But somehow, I healed. Some way, I kept going. And I developed a special place in my heart for women suffering from the types of loss I had endured. I was able to comfort these women in a special way— because of my past, because of what I had been through.

The Mothers Against Drunk Driving (MADD) organization was founded by a mother whose daughter was killed by a drunk driver. This grieving mother found a way to keep moving in the flow of life, which no longer included her daughter, and found a new purpose for her own life.

If the company where you worked for twenty years shuts down, you have to let it die and trust that Destiny is calling you into a new situation. When your marriage ends after all of your efforts to keep it alive, you have to keep going with the flow of Destiny. When you realize a situation cannot be saved, let go and open yourself to the new opportunities.

Amazing Lord: Give me all I need to make it through

this season. Help me to comfort another along the way so that my journey won't be in vain.

91 Faith to Keep Going

〰〰〰〰〰〰〰〰〰〰〰〰〰〰〰〰〰〰〰〰〰〰〰〰〰〰〰〰〰〰〰〰〰〰〰〰〰〰〰

Jesus responded to them, "Have faith in God!

Mark 11:22 (CEB)

I know. I feel like I was knocked down so many times—my husband, my child, my sudden new status as David's wife, the rumors, even the attempts to overthrow my son's throne. I often wondered how I could keep going.

I focused on all God would have for me. I was forced to think about the future and all I had to contribute—to others, to my son, to the promise of his future. It helped to focus forward rather than on the present hurt. I kept going. I kept focusing. I made it.

When you are in a bad place and wondering how you will ever get to your destiny, it takes a lot to get up and keep going. Destiny can seem far off and out of focus when life hits you hard. You feel lost. You feel drained. And the pain can seem overwhelming. But if you want to meet your destiny, you're going to have to get up and get moving—even if you still feel the pain. I'm not saying to ignore your needs. Seek help when needed, but focusing on your pain can make it seem stronger. What you focus on is what you will feel. What you keep your mind staid on is what will drive you.

I suggest you focus on what lies ahead, and then believe in God's power to take you there. You don't have to see the entire plan; you don't even have to know how you will get there. Focus on the future, not the present pain. Trust and believe that God is able to bring you through and bring you to the place designed especially for you—your destiny.

Immanuel, God with Us: Give me strength to focus on the place you would have me to go. Give me faith to believe you will take me there somehow.

92 Know Myself

xxxxxxxxxxxxxxxxxxxxxxxxxxxxxxxxxxxxxxxxxxxxxxxxxxxxxxxxxxxxxxxxxxxxxxxxxxxx

O LORD, you have examined my heart
and know everything about me.
You know when I sit down or stand up.
You know my thoughts even when I'm far away.
You see me when I travel
and when I rest at home.
You know everything I do.

Psalm 139:1-3 (NLT)

You may ask the age-old questions others have asked: why didn't I speak out against the wrong King David did to me and my husband (2 Samuel 11)? Why did I remain silent? Part of the reason is because I really didn't have a voice, women did not speak for themselves, and nobody could speak against the king. I had pretty much lived life as others told me to; from my father's house to my hus-

band Uriah's house then to King David's home. I was always following other people's agenda.

Because of the tragedy surrounding my husband's death and the death of my child, I slowly gained my voice. I realized how dangerous things got all because I didn't stand up or speak out. Now, I don't know if I could have changed things by speaking out, but I needed to know who I was. I examined myself. I examined my motives. I relied on God and prayed and prayed. I learned who I was and what I was called to do. And when given another momentous chance to stand up and speak, I did it. My destiny was at stake and I had learned the dangers of being silent.

In your pursuit of Destiny may you discover what a fascinating person you are. I hope you discover that you are an amazing and unique creation of God. As you get to know yourself, I pray you find out some things you want to change, but you also will discover some things you like about you. Self-discovery can be a deeply rewarding life process, as you learn to embrace truths that others told you about yourself and release the lies that beat down your self-esteem. Enjoy learning about you on this journey.

Bright Morning Star: Give me the wisdom and courage to know myself. Help me to spend valuable time thinking and processing and assessing and praying so that I may discover the amazing and unique person you created.

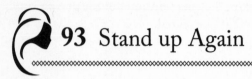# 93 Stand up Again

. . . for though the righteous fall seven times, they rise again . . . .
Proverbs 24:16 (NIV)

I heard it repeated over and over again: how I was taken by David and my husband was killed and my child died. Some people like knowing you as the victim. They like that story.

But rarely do you hear people tell the other part of my story. I got up. I changed my mourning clothes into praise cloth. I overcame. I raised the next king. I participated in the succession process that pointed to the eternal throne of the kingdom. How many times do you hear that story? Whether they tell that story or not, it is what happened. I got up. I stood up. And I kept going toward my destiny.

A Destiny chaser soon realizes that she will have to encourage herself if she is going to make it on this journey. While your friends may want to cheer you on and a few family members might be supportive, the ultimate encouragement will need to come from inside. What you say to yourself and how you see your story will matter much more than what others will say.

Do you see yourself as a victor, an overcomer, the one who can get back up no matter how hard you're knocked down? That's how those who live out their destiny view themselves. Be the victorious hero or heroine of your own story.

Strong and Mighty God: Remind me to stay focused on you as I journey toward my destiny. Give me the courage and strength to stand up no matter what happens.

Bathsheba's Destiny Steps

Decide to focus on your purpose rather than pain today.

Conduct a self-assessment; and check to see if fear, anxiety, or insecurity might be keeping you from choosing exposure.

Determine to walk forth in anticipation of morning's light

What has not worked out according to your plan? Think of a new path and work around your obstacle.

Mary's Story

Luke 1:26-38 (NLT)

In the sixth month of Elizabeth's pregnancy, God sent the angel Gabriel to Nazareth, a village in Galilee, to a virgin named Mary. She was engaged to be married to a man named Joseph, a descendant of King David. Gabriel appeared to her and said, "Greetings, favored woman! The Lord is with you!"

Confused and disturbed, Mary tried to think what the angel could mean. "Don't be afraid, Mary," the angel told her, "for you have found favor with God! You will conceive and give birth to a son, and you will name him Jesus. He will be very great and will be called the Son of the Most High. The Lord God will give him the throne of his ancestor David. And he will reign over Israel forever; his Kingdom will never end!"

Mary asked the angel, "But how can this happen? I am a virgin."

The angel replied, "The Holy Spirit will come upon you, and the power of the Most High will overshadow you. So the baby to be born will be holy, and he will be called the Son of God. What's more, your relative

Elizabeth has become pregnant in her old age! People used to say she was barren, but she has conceived a son and is now in her sixth month. For the word of God will never fail."

Mary responded, "I am the Lord's servant. May everything you have said about me come true." And then the angel left her.

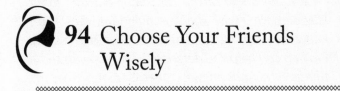 **94** Choose Your Friends
Wisely

*A few days later Mary hurried to the hill country of Judea, to the
town where Zechariah lived. She entered the house and greeted
Elizabeth. At the sound of Mary's greeting, Elizabeth's child leaped
within her, and Elizabeth was filled with the Holy Spirit.*

*Elizabeth gave a glad cry and exclaimed to Mary, "God has blessed
you above all women, and your child is blessed. Why am I so honored, that the mother of my Lord should visit me?"*

Luke 1:39-43 (NLT)

When you know you are called to a certain destiny,
you are very careful about the people with whom
you share your dreams. When I found out I was carrying the Savior of the world, I was overcome with
joy and fear and excitement. Somehow, I was chosen to bear the one who would bring salvation to all

who believed. I knew better than to run and tell the town folk—they wouldn't believe me any way. I ran to my cousin, Elizabeth, for a few reasons.

One, the angel of the Lord had told me about Elizabeth's miracle. She was pregnant, too! And I knew the angel had told me about her for a reason. Praying can help you determine who you can share things with. And I knew Elizabeth's spirit. She wasn't the type of person to get jealous when you had something she didn't. She wasn't the type to spread gossip and talk negatively about people. She was an encourager. She was a sharer of dreams.

I chose to run to visit my cousin Elizabeth because of who she was; and I knew she'd be in my corner, cheering me on to reach my destiny. I could tell by the way she greeted me that she would give me love and support. She was honored that I'd come to visit her. And she reaffirmed me as the one God had chosen to deliver the Savior. What a blessing to have such an encouraging and affirming person in my life during that call to my destiny.

Take a look around you and assess who you have in your corner. With whom can you share your destiny—the inkling you have inside of you? Who would tell you to go for it? Who would pray for you as you deliver on your destiny? Those are the people who you can share your dreams with, and those are the people that you should surround yourself with.

You may have to let go of old friends who are still on the same old stuff—or limit your time with them. Or perhaps you need to cancel a few appointments with the naysayers in your life and add a few more with positive, life-affirming people. The negative thinkers may be distracting you from your destiny. Following your destiny is not always easy, so you need to be around supporters, prayer warriors, and encouragers.

Almighty and Wonderful God: I seek discernment in knowing who to share my dreams and thoughts with. Grant me a circle of supportive and affirming people to journey with toward my destiny.

95 Faith and Transition

∞∞

"For nothing will be impossible with God." Then Mary said, "Here am I, the servant of the Lord; let it be with me according to your word." Then the angel departed from her.

Luke 1:37-38 (ESV)

The day I found out that my destiny was different from what I had planned, I had to make a shift in my thinking and accept the new path that was being presented to me. I was about to get married and start a new life with Joseph. I had no idea that those plans would include a baby—even before we were married. When the angel delivered the news of my destiny, he also said that nothing is impossible with God. I took those words to heart. And when I really let those words sink in, I had only one response: "Okay. Lord, let your will be done. If you say it's going to be done, I'll have the faith to play my part."

I could have focused on all of the possible outcomes—especially the negative ones. What would people say? What would Joseph say? What would my parents say? But at the end of the day, all I needed to remember was what God said. That's how I was able to handle the change in my plans—with faith that God would do just what God said. I was ready to meet my destiny.

Faith is especially needed when you are facing transition. And on the journey toward your destiny, things will change and shift and move—and you cannot plan for all of those changes. There's a verse in a hymn that reminds me of how quickly life changes: *Time is filled with swift transition . . . . Build your hope on things eternal. Hold to God's unchanging hands.*

Life changes. Your plans will change. When we have faith in God to lead us each step of the way, we can accept changes easier. When we know God has an ultimate plan for us and a desire to see us live our destiny, we do not have to fear change. In fact, we can gladly embrace change with the same faith as Mary.

You may not have all of the answers today, but if you follow God's leading, you can let go of anxiety and walk toward your destiny with expectation and certainty. You, too, can say: "Let it be with me according to your word."

Sovereign and Faithful God: I step forward in faith, embracing each change of my plans with anticipation. I know you are taking me closer to my destiny, and I am grateful.

96 Don't Fight Everything

〰〰

But Mary kept all these things, and pondered them in her heart.

Luke 2:19 (KJV)

"Be still, and know that I am God! I will be honored by every nation. I will be honored throughout the world."

Psalm 46:10 (NLT)

The circumstances around Jesus' birth caused a big stir—and for good reason. The angels sang out, the shepherds came looking for us, declarations were made, and people were in an uproar. A Savior was born. And while everyone was not happy nor did everyone believe, the birth of my son caused an uproar. But instead of getting caught up in the pandemonium, I went to a place inside of myself and I pondered what was going on. I remained quiet and simply observed.

As people wondered and speculated about the Destiny I had birthed, I soaked it all in. I watched very carefully. I observed all that was going on and all that was being said, but I didn't feel the need to make a scene or share my thoughts or even tell the people what the angel of the Lord had told me. I was still. I pondered in my heart all that was going on. I didn't think I needed to respond.

Everything said to or about me just didn't need a response. Everything didn't need to be confronted or debated or disputed. My coping mechanism was simple. I remembered what the angel had told me, and I kept all the things I observed in my heart. I knew something great was in the making. I knew Jesus had a destiny all his own—for our salvation. But at that moment, I just didn't feel the need to say a thing.

Silence can be golden. Meditation can bring you peace. Sit back, relax, ponder, and watch God work things out. Fighting keeps you strong, but all of life cannot be spent in fight mode. People who are always fighting run the risk of dying early from strokes and heart attacks. There are times when you need to put down the armor and let your spirit be at rest. Breathe. Release. Relax. Refocus on God and what you have been called to do. Every battle is not yours to fight, and you don't want to wear yourself out going after every issue.

Remembering what God has called you to and why can help you keep your mind on the main thing. It can help you know what is worth fighting for and when to go after it. Peace brings with it a renewal of mind and spirit and body. Peace helps you refocus and helps you refresh so you can fight when you need to and work hard when you have to.

Develop habits that can release you from fight mode and give you much needed breaks. Consider meditation, yoga, or brisk walks to help maintain healthy boundaries and solicit peace. And most importantly, sit still and remember that God is in control and able and willing to bring about your destiny.

Prince of Peace: I seek your guidance in knowing when to fight and when to sit back and ponder all you've promised. Help me to release and renew so that I can reach my destiny.

97 Keep My Eyes on Destiny

xxxxxxxxxxxxxxxxxxxxxxxxxxxxxxxxxxxxxxxxxxxxxxxxxxxxxxxxxxxxxxxxxxxxxxxxxxxxxx

When his parents saw him, they were astonished. His mother said to him, "Son, why have you treated us like this? Your father and I have been anxiously searching for you."

"Why were you searching for me?" he asked. "Didn't you know I had to be in my Father's house?" But they did not understand what he was saying to them. Then he went down to Nazareth with them and was obedient to them. But his mother treasured all these things in her heart. And Jesus grew in wisdom and stature, and in favor with God and man.

Luke 2:48-52 (NIV)

I had a few memory lapses as I raised the Savior of the world. Every now and then I forgot what my part in this life-changing script was. I was just like any other parent. I wanted the best for my son. I wanted to keep him safe in this dangerous world.

When we "lost" young Jesus for a little while, we

panicked. We looked everywhere for him; of course, he was in the temple, listening to the teachers of the law and asking them questions. He had not forgotten his destiny; he knew he had to be about God's business. But me, I was just concerned about my child. I let anxiety and worry cause me to forget what Jesus' purpose was and what mine was, too. When Jesus told me he had to be about God's business, I instantly snapped back to reality.

I was nurturing and raising the Savior of the world. I had been told. I knew what to expect. Why was I worrying? I treasured the happenings of those days in my heart and remembered what God had called me to do. I was once again able to be about my business of taking care of Jesus and watching him grow.

Following the road to your destiny takes focus. When you take your eyes off of the prize, you can get frustrated and disoriented; you can forget what you are supposed to be doing. If you keep your eyes on the road to Destiny, your life will follow. When you remember what you are called to do, what you are created for, you can better follow your mission during trying times.

Taking your eyes off of your purpose can cause you to get distracted, discouraged, or anxious. You may wonder why somethings are happening; you may fret about some signs on the way. But the best medicine for anxiety is to recall, remember, and recommit to the path God has called you to follow.

Be aware of forgetting your true purpose and real destiny. Your memory lapse can cause you to panic and worry unnecessarily. What you are experiencing could just be a lesson on the road to your destiny—and you'll miss it because you are caught up in the anxiety. Stop and think about God's promises. Stop and observe what is going on around you.

By trusting God's plans for you to meet your destiny, you will be able to keep going—even when there is fear or there are complications. You can press on with your purpose in mind and your eyes fixed on Destiny.

Precious Lord: Guide me as I journey toward my destiny. Keep my eyes focused on your plans for my life so I can keep walking along the path you have designed for me.

98 Life and Death

~~~~~~

When Jesus saw his mother there and the disciple whom he loved standing nearby, he said to his mother, "Dear woman, here is your son," and to the disciple, "Here is your mother." From this time on, this disciple took her into his home.

John 19:26-27 (NIV)

Death swallowed by triumphant Life! Who got the last word, oh, Death? Oh, Death, who's afraid of you now?

1 Corinthians 15:55 (MSG)

I learned a valuable lesson about death while raising the Son of Man and listening to him while he was gifted to us on earth. I had the privilege to be called Mary, the Mother of God. I had the honor of delivering the baby Jesus, who was both human and divine. I had the unbelievable task and opportunity to watch this child grow and gain knowledge and wisdom and fulfill the very mission he was put on earth to accomplish. I had a front-row seat to the ultimate example of living your destiny.

So when the day came for my son to die, I was sad. But I didn't grieve like one without hope (1 Thessalonians 4:13). First, Jesus was always taking care of business, and even on the cross he saw fit to make sure I was okay while on this earth. He looked at his disciple John and told him to take me in as his mother, and he told me to look after John. He made arrangements for both John and me; he took care of us, just like he always does.

But things went even further. Jesus' death wasn't ordinary, not only because he was the Savior and would be resurrected in just three days but because of how he lived his life. He lived for his destiny. He lived according to his purpose. He knew what he was birthed to do, and he did it—very well. Even when it got hard and overwhelming, he prayed and sought God's help. He reminded himself why he was here, and he was renewed and ready to move forward.

Many are afraid of death—death of a loved one and even their own death. But death does not have to be a scary venture when you've lived—really lived—according to your purpose. Jesus was and remains the perfect example of living a fulfilled life. Death did not get the victory because he lived his life on purpose. That's the amazing thing about destiny. We all were created to fulfill some role through which we can only find the great elixir of contentment and courage. Whatever the assignment, death loses its license to threaten those of us who are certain we have lived before we face its clutching grasp.

If you want to face death with certainty and without fear, live today. Live according to your purpose and find your destiny. Give all you've got to find your destiny and live it to the fullest. Then death will lose its hold on you, too. It won't be able to sting the one who has lived well and fulfilled his or her destiny.

Eternal God: Thank you for the reminder to live this life to its fullest, following the path and purpose you've called me to. I am thankful for your eternal plans, and I know I don't have to fear death.

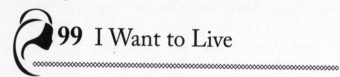

99 I Want to Live

And Mary said: "My soul glorifies the Lord and my spirit rejoices in God my Savior, for he has been mindful of the humble state of his servant. From now on all generations will call me blessed, for the Mighty One has done great things for me—holy is his name."

Luke 1:46-49 (NIV)

When the angel of the Lord appeared to me and told me I would be the mother of Jesus, something inside of me leapt. It could have been the baby, but it was a little early for that. The moment I decided to accept God's plan for my life—without worrying about what the townspeople would say—I truly began to live and my entire being changed. It was then that I discovered what I was put on earth for, and I was glad to receive such a blessing and honor.

I could have rejected what the angel was saying; I could have hidden in fear or bargained with God *to please find another way to bring about the Savior of the world. But I was tired of just existing as a person. I wanted to live with purpose. I'm so happy I was ready to receive the news and to live my life as a co-creator with God, helping to bring about salvation to the entire world. You can see why I rejoiced.*

Real life means discovering who and what God has placed inside of you, and dancing and rejoicing while you let whatever *that* is play out in your life. It takes courage to be the person you were created to be, to live according to instinct, and walk in your destiny. It's not a journey for the weak. But those who refuse to go against the grain and live authentically, failing to answer the call that beckons in their soul, are merely existing. They are clocking in and out, living day-to-day.

But when you are in tune with the "why" of life—why God placed you on this earth—you begin to live. You can work with joy. You can walk throughout the day, reciting the words of Mary: "My soul glorifies the Lord and my spirit rejoices in God my Savior." Real life means discovering what God has placed inside of you. Real joy comes from doing whatever that is.

God has invested a great deal in you. And for all the Creator has put in you, there is only one thing God wants to know: "What will you do with what I gave you?" God expects you to work excellence at the level given you. As the late author, professor, and motivational speaker Leo Buscaglia explained it, "Your talent is God's gift to you. What you do with it is your gift back to God." And that is living!

Great Giver of Life: My soul rejoices in knowing you have created me with a specific purpose in mind. My spirit delights in you and your awesome plan.

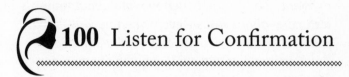

100 Listen for Confirmation

She came along just as Simeon was talking with Mary and Joseph, and she began praising God. She talked about the child to everyone who had been waiting expectantly for God to rescue Jerusalem.

Luke 2:38 (NLT)

One thing I thank God for on my journey is the ability to listen. I don't know if I could have borne this cross as Jesus' mother without having confirmations from God. From the very beginning, God sent me signs that I was raising a special child. From conception on throughout his life on earth, God reminded me that Jesus was the Savior. And I thank God I was able to hear those messages and receive them. I was open and aware of the messages God sent and I believed. I needed to hang on to the confirmations, especially when the road got tough and my destiny seemed like a bitter pill.

When I saw how people mistreated my son, I could rely on the things God had allowed me to see. I could believe the things God had deposited in my spirit about Jesus. I often thought about Anna's testimony about Jesus—even when he was just a young child (Luke 2:36-38). Her words reminded me that God was doing something beyond comprehension in Jesus and that I just needed to trust the process, to trust God's strategy. I thank God for ears to hear and a heart to listen.

When God gives you a strategy, you can overcome. Be patient. Be discerning and wait on God's strategies. You can't meet up with Destiny without one. You can have resources—but having resources without a strategy is how lottery winners end up broke. You can have opportunities—but an opportunity without a strategy won't sustain itself. When you meet up with Destiny, you want it to be for the long haul so having a godly strategy will give you what you need.

When you humble yourself and let God know that you don't know, you can watch God reveal things to you—directly, through others, and in many other ways. You make room to receive what God has for you when you are in listening mode. Maybe that is why some things happen—to bring us to our knees, to get ourselves out of the way, and to open our ears and hearts to God's divine plan for our lives.

Wonderful Counselor: I love you and appreciate your helping me to hear your voice. Remind me of your messages as I move forward to reach my destiny.

 **101** Only God Sees the
Big Picture

◇◇◇

When Jesus had finished telling these stories and illustrations, he left that part of the country. He returned to Nazareth, his hometown. When he taught there in the synagogue, everyone was amazed and said, "Where does he get this wisdom and the power to do miracles?"

Matthew 13:53-54 (NLT)

When people saw Jesus living out his mission and destiny, they didn't get it. They knew him as the baby born to me in a lowly manger. They knew him as the little one who used to run around with Joseph and me. These people only could see what their eyes allowed them to; they couldn't see the full picture of God's plan for me or for Jesus.

It used to bother me when they talked badly about my child, but I realize that it wasn't their job to see the big picture. They didn't have the vision, and I couldn't let their words and actions get to me or stop me from believing what God had already revealed to me. Their words weren't going to stop God's plan—so I just let them say whatever they had to say and I kept remembering God's words to me.

Opinions can be positive, but nobody on the road to their destiny can afford to get caught up in the opinions of others. People will love you, but can quickly turn against you. When you're positioned toward Destiny, don't get caught in the false lure of popularity. Develop a thick skin even when you're popular, and don't believe your own resume. Otherwise, it can later be painful to hear cruel, deconstructive criticism. You cannot have it both ways: you can't choose to hear only the voices of those who adore you and shut down the voices of those who don't.

Your destiny doesn't depend on the opinions of haters—or applauders, either. They're all making judgments about your future based on your right now, and that's not a complete picture. Only God sees the big picture. Stay focused on the God-given plans and you will succeed—no matter what others say.

Heavenly Helper: Forgive me for getting caught up in the opinions of others. Keep me focused on you and your directions. I know only you can see the big picture.

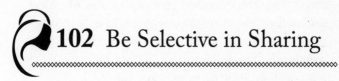

102 Be Selective in Sharing

Mary stayed with Elizabeth for three months and then went back to her own home.

Luke 1:56 (MSG)

Now to him who by the power at work within us is able to accomplish abundantly far more than all we can ask or imagine, to him be glory in the church and in Christ Jesus to all generations, forever and ever. Amen.

Ephesians 3:20-21 (NRSV)

I felt led to visit my cousin Elizabeth—and to stay for three months. Elizabeth had always been welcoming and encouraging, and she had a bit of her own miracle-making news to share. She was aware of how God could use an ordinary person to do something absolutely mind blowing and amazing. She personally knew how God could answer prayers *that others thought were impossible.*

I chose to share with Elizabeth and to sit in her company. It's what I needed at that time; it kept me away from the eyes and ears and voices of others and helped me to celebrate my world-altering destiny, too. I thank God for Elizabeth. I thank God for a cousin who I could share my dreams with. I couldn't tell everyone, but I told the right one.

Sometimes when you are trying to reach your destiny, you've got to learn to keep your mouth shut. It's not like you're going to be secretive or sneaky, but everyone just can't see the vision—and sometimes you need to either be around supporters or by yourself.

Are you lagging behind in fulfilling your destiny because you're listening to negative voices? Learn to be selective about who you share your dreams with. Some can't handle it. People with low aims can actually cause you to feel guilty or foolish for daring to have a dream. And people who may want different things out of life can make you feel bad for wanting what you desire. Nothing is wrong with what they want. Nothing is wrong with what you want. That you dare to have different dreams can scare people, especially those in your comfort zone. When you encounter these reactions, make a mental note to protect your dream from such persons and understand that the reason for their fright, anger, or intimidation has nothing to do with you or what you are destined to do.

Precious Lamb of God: I desire to be surrounded by helpful supporters who can encourage me to meet my destiny as I encourage them to meet theirs. Show me who I can trust.

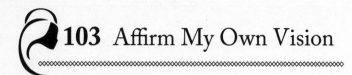

103 Affirm My Own Vision

"And did you know that your cousin Elizabeth conceived a son, old as she is? Everyone called her barren, and here she is six months pregnant! Nothing, you see, is impossible with God."

And Mary said, "Yes, I see it all now: I'm the Lord's maid, ready to serve. Let it be with me just as you say."

Luke 1:36-38 (MSG)

Once the angel delivered the news to me, letting me know that God had chosen me to give birth to the Savior, I began to see myself as the mother of the Son of God. I said it—right after I got over the shock. I didn't fully understand everything and how it would work out, but I did understand that nothing is impossible with God. So instead of fretting over how and why and what, I praised God.

I started walking as the mother of Jesus right then and there. I didn't have the child in my arms yet, but I began to see myself as his mother. I began to prepare myself for this journey. I knew it would include some pain and heartache, but I also knew that this was a part of my destiny. I envisioned it. I lived it. I fulfilled it. Thanks be to God.

Vision is important when going after your destiny; and you need to imagine what God is doing in your life—even before it happens. Spend time talking with yourself about what Destiny holds for your future. Hear your own voice affirm your vision. See yourself in the place you desire to be.

If you're not living your destiny as you journey, you won't be able to live it after you reach your destination. Destiny is not only a destination, a goal, a dream, a purpose; it is an inner process of becoming all you were meant to be. Your mind is already where you were called to be while you await the actual fulfillment. Join in with Mary and proclaim: "I see it now; nothing is impossible with God."

Light of the World: I see it now. I know what you have called me to and I know it will come to pass. Help me

enjoy the journey as I reach my destination, giving you praise and glory each step of the way.

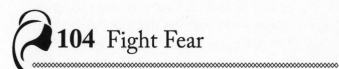104 Fight Fear

XXXXXXXXXXXXXXXXXXXXXXXXXXXXXXXXXXXXXXXXXXXXXXXXXXXXXXXXXXXXXXXX

Upon entering, Gabriel greeted her: Good morning! You're beautiful
with God's beauty, Beautiful inside and out! God be with you. She
was thoroughly shaken, wondering what was behind a greeting like
that. But the angel assured her, "Mary, you have nothing to fear.
God has a surprise for you: You will become pregnant and give birth
to a son and call his name Jesus.

Luke 1:28-31 (MSG)

For God hath not given us the spirit of fear; but of power, and of
love, and of a sound mind.

2 Timothy 1:7 (KJV)

I know it seems like I quickly accepted God's will for
me to be the mother of the man Jesus, but I was
fearful—especially in the beginning. I considered
it a joy and a privilege to be chosen as the mother
of Jesus, but I was also startled when the angel of
God approached me. This was a lot to take in. And it

wasn't every day one was visited by the angel of the Lord with a message. When the angel first greeted me, saying I was favored by God, I was fearful.

But thanks be to God, I accepted my calling and my destiny. I eased into this new position and embraced all that came with it. I stayed close to God. I recalled all of God's promises, and I learned to fight my fear so I could enjoy this amazing blessing. I wanted to enjoy every moment toward my destiny and Jesus' destiny to save the world! When fear tried to creep in and ruin my journey, I fought it. I focused on the mission.

When the discomfort of your new environment makes you fearful, ride the wave of feelings long enough to give it a good test-drive. Your initial fight-or-flight response may tell you to run for your life, but determine to engage your "fight" response and stay exposed to your new situation until your comfort level increases. Fight through feelings of inadequacy and own the new space.

You will never know what joy or what lessons you could have encountered in your new space if you decide to run too early. I'm not saying that every new place needs to be your resting place, but don't let fear be the reason you leave prematurely. Let each season run its course so you can receive all you were destined to gain during that time and in that place.

Author and Finisher of My Faith: I will not allow fear to make me run from the new things in my life and on my path. I will release the spirit of fear and walk in your way in faith.

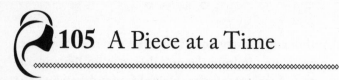

105 A Piece at a Time

But do not forget this one thing, dear friends: With the Lord a day is like a thousand years, and a thousand years are like a day.

2 Peter 3:8 (NIV)

When the angel of the Lord approached me and told me that I was going to bring forth the Savior of the World, I took the news in stride. Yes, I was shocked. Yes, I was stunned. Yes, I was honored. According to the angel, I was chosen for a phenomenal job and I had an amazing destiny to grasp. But what would have happened if the angel would have laid out all of the details right there for me—letting me know the trouble we'd go through when I was about to have the baby, how King Herod would put a hit out on my child, how the people would treat my son, and how he'd eventually go about destroying the power of sin in the world. You know how this thing

culminates—the resurrection is amazing; but let's
be honest, the crucifixion and all that led up to it
was inhumane.

Imagine if I would have known all of these details
during that fateful day when I found out my place
in this play. I may have not been ready. I may not
have been so joyous and exuberant. My song may
have turned to a dirge. I would not have been able
to give hope to so many—if I had known all that
would transpire.

God knows just how much we can bear. God knows how much to share with each of us on this journey. If God showed you what the Almighty really had in store for you right from the beginning, it might scare you into a corner from which you might never reappear. Therefore, God has to reveal our destiny to us in pieces.

God created you and knows what you have the capacity to do—but you don't. You may see yourself as just a chemistry student or merely a mechanic. God sees the passion inside of you that goes far beyond your present circumstances. God sees the great inventor, entrepreneur, physician, or teacher that you can become in time. If God showed you what your Creator really sees in you, you probably couldn't handle it. So you get a little bit of it at a time. You have so much to learn along the journey that you receive it in stages.

Almighty and Amazing God: I am eternally grateful that you reign supreme and know exactly what I can handle. Thank you for revealing all I need to know right now. I will walk in faith knowing you have the full picture in view.

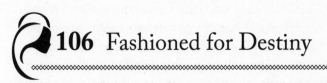

106 Fashioned for Destiny

Then GOD's Message came to me: "Can't I do just as this potter does, people of Israel?" GOD's Decree! "Watch this potter. In the same way that this potter works his clay, I work on you, people of Israel."

Jeremiah 18:5-6 (MSG)

Even though the angel of the Lord spoke to me and shared my destiny with me, I didn't fully understand it or see the entire picture unroll in front of my face. I picked up glimpses of my destiny along the way— and that was just fine with me.

God must have known I needed time to fully digest this role as the mother of Jesus. I needed time to understand how my little baby would grow and become so loved and so hated at the same time. Lord knows, I needed time to grow into a patient and understanding woman. I would never have been able to stand at the cross watching the blood stream down my child's body if God had not been working on me throughout my life.

From the faith of my relatives, like Elizabeth, to the shepherds song and wise men's visit, to Simeon and Anna's proclamations and so many signs during Jesus' ministry, I was given just a piece of information to let me know I was in the right place and Jesus was in the right place. We were walking in Destiny and God was preparing me to receive the fullness of that Destiny—one step at a time.

Sometimes you get exposed to a business as an intern before you become CEO. Perhaps your exposure to the life of a district attorney comes while you are working your way through law school. Your introduction to having your own landscaping business may begin with you cutting lawns in the neighborhood. Your career as a solo artist may launch with you singing in the church choir. Each opportunity then builds on the last until you become fully ready to stand in the position to which Destiny calls you.

When Destiny unfolds rather than explodes in front of us, we can have a greater understanding of where we have been and where we are going. Having full knowledge of all the Almighty has in store for us would probably freak us out. The self we see now is not the person the Creator will shape to receive Destiny.

Gracious and Merciful God: I know you are shaping me and molding me into the person you would have me to be. You are getting me ready to meet my destiny.

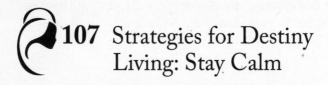

107 Strategies for Destiny Living: Stay Calm

Do you see what this means—all these pioneers who blazed the way, all these veterans cheering us on? It means we'd better get on with it. Strip down, start running—and never quit!

Hebrews 12:1-2 (MSG)

Many people want to know how I managed to stay so calm while walking in my destiny. After all, I did witness the brutal attacks on my son's character, the plot to kill him in the worse possible way, the betrayal by his close friends—it was a lot to endure and to see. But I never let those things rattle me. I didn't focus on the horrific things happening; I focused on what I knew was true: Jesus had come to transform the world; Jesus had come to change the world's view of what it looked like to have God's kingdom here on earth. I stayed calm because I stayed fo-

cused on Jesus' purpose—and my purpose.

When I was tempted to fret or worry, I remembered the stories of the people who had come before me—how they endured by faith. I remembered how my cousin Elizabeth had endured all she went through by faith. I thought about the amazing events surrounding Jesus' birth and what the shepherds told me when they visited. I thought about meeting Simeon and Anna in the temple when we dedicated Jesus. Oh, things got crazy and dramatic, but I was able to stay calm because I stayed focused on the ultimate destiny.

When you take a survey of folks who are actively engaged with their destiny, you can find some common strands. I like to call these tendencies, strategies—the things Destiny followers have in common when living their lives to the fullest.

First and foremost, those who are intent on following their destiny don't feed on drama. These are not the people you see screaming and having emotional meltdowns every time they run into a problem. They've learned to stay calm regardless of what is happening. Horror movies are intended to be overly dramatic to entice your emotions. Notice, those who die in a horror flick are the ones who scream and freak out. They feed into the drama. When you are attacked on your Destiny journey, don't give in to that drama in your life.

Think about how you've overcome in the past; use your cloud of witnesses—those who have successfully journeyed before you (Hebrews 11) and who are still journeying before you—to gain strength and perspective. Stay calm in the midst of the storm. Keep Calm! God is in control; your destiny is just ahead.

My Savior and My Strength: I will remain calm no matter what happens. I know you have called me for a purpose and will give me all I need to fulfill your calling. I will not focus on what is going on around me, but instead I will look to you and my cloud of witnesses.

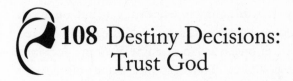

108 Destiny Decisions: Trust God

∞∞∞∞∞∞∞∞∞∞∞∞∞∞∞∞∞∞∞∞∞∞∞∞∞∞∞∞∞∞∞∞∞∞∞∞∞∞∞

Trust in the LORD with all your heart, and do not rely on your own insight. In all your ways acknowledge [the LORD], and [God] will make straight your paths.

Proverbs 3:5-6 (NRSV)

I was able to walk in my destiny—even in the roughest days—because I trusted God. This trust alone got me through so many trials and tribulations. This trust alone got me to walk each day with renewed purpose and renewed joy because I knew I was doing what God had planned. Even the rumors and whispers from people—some from my own relatives—didn't stop me from walking in my destiny; they couldn't.

From the day that angel shared the news of my destiny with me, I decided to trust God completely *with all parts of the plan. I am thankful to God for being faithful and trustworthy.*

Some decisions don't have an impact on your destiny. It won't matter whether you put on black socks or brown socks today. You can drive a red car or a silver one, a sedan or an SUV. Some decisions are inconsequential choices, so please don't place yourself under pressure by thinking every decision has to be carefully crafted, lest your destiny be lost. Make the choices you want and enjoy your life.

But you *will* have to make some decisions that are pivotal to Destiny. These choices will make the critical difference between your ability to arrive at Destiny or not. These decisions will have an impact on the rest of your life.

Destiny decisions have a price. I'm not necessarily talking about a monetary cost, although financial choices often have an impact on Destiny. Most often the cost is courage in interpersonal relationships. It takes courage to make Destiny decisions. You need courage to ignore what Grandma wants you to do with your life and choose Destiny. Your Destiny decision may cost you Uncle Willie's approval. Your Destiny choices may cause you to lose some people you regarded as friends.

What are you going to do with the life you have left? You may have fifty years or you may have two, but find the courage to make Destiny choices for the time you have. Begin with trusting God through this process. When you commit to following the path God is calling you to, you gain assurance that God will lead and guide you each step of the way. This assurance can help you make decisions that may seem tough to others, but you know they are in line with your destiny. Make the decision to begin with trusting God.

God Almighty: I trust you with my life. I trust you to guide me to my destiny. I know you are faithful and trustworthy.

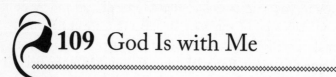

109 God Is with Me

So, what do you think? With God on our side like this, how can we lose?

Romans 8:31 (MSG)

I really was never one for big crowds. I learned early in life that people are only with you for a minute—then they turn on you, often times criticizing your dreams and visions. Because I was given a special destiny, I felt as if I needed to guard it against negativity. I couldn't stop the people from talking and hating, but I could stop myself from listening and focusing on their words.

I moved to a new place—mentally. I recalled the words of the angel of the Lord and the words of those who confirmed my calling. I learned to remind myself that God was with me and I could not lose. God hadn't brought me to this new world and new life to leave me. I had a destiny and I needed to get there—regardless of what others said.

If you're going to move from your comfort zone to your creative zone, you're going to have to tune out others and tune into God and your inner voice that reminds you of all you were created to do and empowered to do. In the creative zone, you're not always going to have cheerleaders; you're going to have to be your biggest cheerleader.

Because comfort zoners like sameness, if they find your ideas distasteful that may be your green light to keep moving forward. Jump fully into the creative zone, and you will find fulfillment and purpose that you cannot imagine as a comfort zone dweller. If you've been banned from the comfort zone of your friends, job, or neighborhood, say, "Goodbye and good riddance!" Have the courage to walk away from them even if they scare you with warnings of dire consequences or potential pitfalls of taking risks and doing something differently.

While Destiny calls you, friends, loved ones, and co-workers in the comfort zone will tell you to be afraid to go back to school, to fear quitting your job to start a business, or that you aren't creative enough to write music or plays or books. At such times, you will need to "encourage yourself." Remind yourself why you started this journey toward Destiny and that God is right by your side—and keep it moving forward.

Immanuel, God with Us: I know you are right by my side. I know you won't let me fail. I will focus on you and not the words of others.

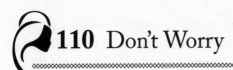

110 Don't Worry

◇◇

Don't fret or worry. Instead of worrying, pray. Let petitions and praises shape your worries into prayers, letting God know your concerns. Before you know it, a sense of God's wholeness, every-thing coming together for good, will come and settle you down. It's wonderful what happens when Christ displaces worry at the center of your life.

Philippians 4:6-7 (MSG)

Jesus' father and mother were speechless with surprise at these words. Simeon went on to bless them, and said to Mary his mother, This child marks both the failure and the recovery of many in Israel, A figure misunderstood and contradicted—the pain of a sword-thrust through you—But the rejection will force honesty, as God reveals who they really are.

Luke 2:33-35 (MSG)

Being chosen as the mother of Christ was a hum-bling and joyous honor; but as you already know, this calling didn't come without sacrifice and pain. Many have wondered how I handled knowing that Jesus would grow up to be rejected, abused, and even put to death. How does a mother watch silently as her child enters a danger zone, knowing that his destiny will present life-altering challenges that no one else has experienced? How could I still consider myself as one favored by God when I knew all Jesus would endure—and that I'd be right there watching it go down. Yes, I birthed the Savior. But I'd also watch him die. Yes, God had already promised that he'd be resurrected, but watching him die on the cross was still very real and very painful. How did I survive?

I believed. I believed what God had shown me through the prophets. I believed what God's Word said about the coming of the Savior. And then I turned all of that information and my concerns over to God. I prayed and prayed and prayed. I sang praises to God for all he had done and all he was doing. My mind focused on the outcome and God's faithfulness—not the situation. Eventually, I wasn't worried anymore. I was able to trust God, to believe that what God said would come to pass, and that it would be okay. I didn't let pain of what was happening overrule the joy and honor of being Jesus' mother. I didn't let my worry crowd out the promises of God. I lived in peace.

In *Instinct*, I write about a special apparatus racehorses wear called blinders. The blinders keep the horses from looking to the left and right to see where the other horses in the race are; in other words, the blinders help the horses stay focused. By focusing on their goal, they don't get distracted by what is going on around them, which could cause them to get discouraged and slow down.

When you are trying to reach your destiny, you will sometimes need to put on mental blinders that serve the same purpose as the horse's blinder. Your mental blinder will need to keep you looking at your purpose and how you will meet up with destiny, not your circumstances or on what others are saying. Circumstances may cause you to worry and fret, but when your mind is focused—on what you are called to do and God's promise of provisions—you can release worry and stress and have more peace and energy to do what you are supposed to be doing. Release the worry. Focus on your goal.

Alpha and Omega: Give me blinders to keep me

focused on my destiny each day. Help me not to get distracted by the circumstances and concerns of the day, but to pray about everything and release it to you. I desire to walk this journey in peace, focusing on your promises and faithfulness.

111 Ordered Steps

※※

And because Joseph was a descendant of King David, he had to go to Bethlehem in Judea, David's ancient home. He traveled there from the village of Nazareth in Galilee. He took with him Mary, his fiancée, who was now obviously pregnant.

And while they were there, the time came for her baby to be born. She gave birth to her first child, a son. She wrapped him snugly in strips of cloth and laid him in a manger, because there was no lodging available for them.

Luke 2:4-7 (NLT)

The LORD directs our steps, so why try to understand everything along the way?

Proverbs 20:24 (NLT)

Throughout the years of following my destiny of taking care of the Savior of the world, I learned to accept the sometimes circular nature of the journey and to trust God. When Joseph told me we needed to take such a long trip while I was close to having my promised child, I was not happy. The trip from Nazareth to Bethlehem could take nearly three days. But instead of letting my emotions take over and getting upset, I got ready and went with him.

Once we got there and I delivered the Savior, I realized that God was working everything out for our good. Our child was born in Bethlehem—as foretold in the Old Testament Scripture.

We can drive ourselves crazy wondering why something happened or trying to force something else to happen the way we think it should or the way we want it to. But Destiny followers realize early on this journey that their steps are truly ordered by God. If God has called you to a task, God will bring you through it and to it. It may not look like you had planned it would, but God is faithful and will bring things to pass—in God's special timing.

So instead of fretting and worrying, trust God. And do your very best. Work your gifts, get your exposure, talk to your mentors, pray, read, research, and enjoy the journey. It can be filled with great adventure—even more than you dream of. It's a part of your destiny.

Gracious and Great God: Thank you for the journey you have set me on. I vow not to get upset or worried when things do not work out as planned. I trust your plans more than my plans.

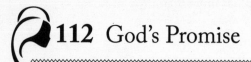

112 God's Promise

xxxxxxxxxxxxxxxxxxxxxxxxxxxxxxxxxxxxxxxxxxxxxxxxxxxxxxxxxxxxxxxxxxxxxxxxxxxx

But now, GOD's Message, the God who made you in the first place, Jacob, the One who got you started, Israel: "Don't be afraid, I've redeemed you. I've called your name. You're mine. When you're in over your head, I'll be there with you. When you're in rough waters, you will not go down. When you're between a rock and a hard place, it won't be a dead end—Because I am GOD, your personal God, The Holy of Israel, your Savior.

Isaiah 43:1-3 (MSG)

I have tried hard to find you—don't let me wander from your commands. I have hidden your word in my heart, that I might not sin against you. I praise you, O LORD; teach me your decrees.

Psalm 119:10-12 (NLT)

Whenever this journey toward my destiny got difficult, I stopped and refocused myself on God's promises. I realized that was the only thing I really could trust. Humans change. I saw this first hand. People

who claimed to be excited about the Savior of the world didn't expect to see a baby born of humble people and in less than royal circumstances. They turned on me and my family and my son. They said awful things and acted even worse. It was tough.

But I remembered the words of God. I knew that God had not brought me to this place to leave me or to destroy me. I had to wait it out and trust that God would bring things to pass, just as God promised. I knew I wouldn't die in those places—even though it felt like I would. I knew God was right there with me and bringing about my deliverance. I would not have been able to make this journey if I hadn't hidden the promises of God in my heart.

Know the promises of God and rely on them to help you get back and up and push forward. Rehearse them, repeat them, sing them—do whatever it takes to keep them front and center in your mind. You will need them to regain strength and refocus for the journey. Your destiny is just ahead.

Faithful Promise Keeper: I am thankful for all of your promises. I will hide your Word in my heart so I can recall your promises and move forward on this journey.

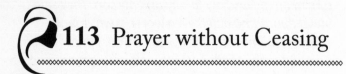

113 Prayer without Ceasing

They all met together and were constantly united in prayer, along with Mary the mother of Jesus, several other women, and the brothers of Jesus.

Acts 1:14 (NLT)

Never stop praying.

1 Thessalonians 5:17 (NLT)

To always pray—or never stop praying—is the secret I found to keep moving toward my destiny. Prayer is what I did when I awoke in the morning, looking toward the new challenges of raising a martyr. Prayer is what I did during the day when I had to deal with people's negative words about my own Son. Prayer is what I did when I knew he would face the ugly execution—crucifixion— the ultimate sacrifice for humankind, And while I understood that *his death wasn't really the end, it was sometimes difficult to live with the reality of Jesus' mission and my mission.*

Prayer got me through. Prayer refocused my mind on the power of God, not the pettiness of people. Prayer gave me hope and peace and joy. I wouldn't have gotten through if I hadn't prayed all the time.

Prayer may seem like a simple part of reaching your destiny, but it has powerful implications. Prayer is really the center of our relationship with God. It is the pipeline that gets us in connection with our source. Since we are created by God and given a destiny by God, we should want to stay in close connection to our Originator. Who better to know how to calm our fears and to push us closer to Destiny than the one who slung the stars in the air and crafted the sensors in our minds to make us all uniquely who we are?

Pray about everything. Pray in the morning, during the day, and at night. Let prayer become as seamless and continuous as your next breath.

Guiding Light: I want to pray without ceasing; I want to pray when I breathe in and when I breathe out. I want this journey to take me closer and closer to you.

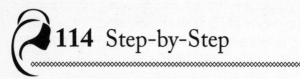

114 Step-by-Step

You're blessed when you stay on course, walking steadily on the road revealed by God. You're blessed when you follow his directions, doing your best to find him.

Psalm 119:1-2 (MSG)

I had the pleasure of watching Jesus grow from an infant to a great man, leader, and teacher for more than thirty-three years. Each of these days and years were not filled with excitement nor were each of these times filled with joy and happiness. There were some lows, and there were some very mediocre days. Most days were pretty mundane.

But I knew what God had said. I knew what Simeon and Anna had said. I knew I was grooming and nurturing the Son of God, who would save the world. I just had to do what I was called to do each day, step-by-step, and I would see the promises of God come to pass. My destiny was connected to what I did each day, whether it was exciting or mundane.

Following the path to Destiny isn't all highs. You don't feel like you're doing something ground-breaking every day. To survive, you have to find joy in knowing you are on a God-ordained path. You find joy in knowing you are doing what you are sup-posed to be doing—even if that means washing the dishes right now or cooking the food or taking care of a seemingly unimportant detail. It all adds up to your destiny; and when you keep that in mind, the boring days can still be blessed, the low days can be lessons, and the high days are just samples of what is to come. Walk steadily with God—each day.

Destiny is about more than simply reaching a desti-nation. What you gain along your way to your destina-tion is part of Destiny. You can't get to Destiny and bypass people, experiences, and lessons. Successes will boost you closer to Destiny, but so will your mistakes. The lessons you learn will drive you nearer to Destiny, but so will the instruction you failed to heed. This com-plex mix is inextricably part of the Destiny process.

Surviving that process requires that you find joy in the details on your path to Destiny: the menial job, demanding boss, failed relationships, and financial set-backs. Keep them in perspective. Recognize that each brings you closer to Destiny.

Remember your strategy during these long, uneventful seasons because it gives you concrete reasons to keep pushing forward. Want your future badly enough to grab hold and not let go when the day-to-day has you bored or feeling like a failure. It is a step-by-step journey.

Bread of Life: I thank you for this day. I thank you for this journey toward my destiny. I will stay close to you each step of the way and find joy in the journey.

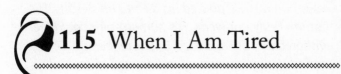115 When I Am Tired

xxxxxxxxxxxxxxxxxxxxxxxxxxxxxxxxxxxxxxxxxxxxxxxxxxxxxxxxxxxxxxxxxxxxxxxxxxxx

[God] gives power to the faint, and strengthens the powerless. Even youths will faint and be weary, and the young will fall exhausted; but those who wait for the LORD shall renew their strength, they shall mount up with wings like eagles, they shall run and not be weary, they shall walk and not faint.

Isaiah 40:29-31 (NRSV)

"Come to me, all you that are weary and are carrying heavy burdens, and I will give you rest. Take my yoke upon you, and learn from me; for I am gentle and humble in heart, and you will find rest for your souls. For my yoke is easy, and my burden is light."

Matthew 11:28-30 (NRSV)

I learned from my son—from what he did and what he said. Jesus told his disciples, those laboring with him, to get away for a little while and get some rest. He encouraged them to renew themselves and their spirits before continuing on the journey.

My son knew firsthand how pursuing your purpose and Destiny takes hard work and effort. Pursuing his destiny revitalized his soul, but it could also wear him out. He poured his all into his destiny. His human body got weak. His human spirit could feel withered and dry and tired. But he renewed his body and soul—by connecting to God, and I followed his example and found hope in sharing my burdens with God, and resting.

Destiny chasers are very often serious about their work—as they should be. When you have been given a vision and a purpose, you want to take off running and meet your destiny. But it is wise to remember that we are humans and our bodies and spirits get weary.

It is okay. Weariness doesn't mean you don't want your vision to come to pass; it probably means you've been working hard. But take a note from Jesus and remember to renew and refresh yourself. Jesus got away and prayed. Jesus encouraged others to break away and regain focus.

Press on, yes. But remember balance, and don't forsake your physical, spiritual, and emotional health when chasing after Destiny. You want to be healthy enough to enjoy the journey and the destination.

Pace yourself. Enjoy the flowers on the road. Enjoy

the people in your life. Enjoy the ride. It's okay to rest. It's how you will be renewed for the next leg of the journey.

Destiny Designer: I come to you, sometimes weary and weak. Renew my strength. Refresh my mind and body so I may continue to run this race and do your will.

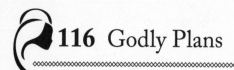

116 Godly Plans

For I know the plans I have for you," says the LORD. "They are plans for good and not for disaster, to give you a future and a hope."
Jeremiah 29:11 (NLT)

I found that frustration particularly crept in when I saw the big picture and the big vision God had for me and Jesus. Along the way, I knew our purpose so well. I could see it and taste it and feel it. I knew the amazing joy it was supposed to bring and a lot about how the amazing salvation story would play out. But the closer we got to fulfilling that mission, sometimes the harder it got.

The reality of the circumstances didn't line up some days with what I knew in my mind and spirit. My vision was clouded by the issues at hand, the negative people, and the trials. I had to find the courage to hang on to God's plans and to see God's *vision, not the circumstances. God's plans were for our good.*

As you strive for Destiny, your vision may function at a higher level than your opportunity, which can create frustration. On the inside, you can feel what is calling to you; yet nothing and no one on the outside validates your feeling. Hold your destiny close to your heart. Keep listening to your own voice. Hold on to your revelation. Keep focusing. Keep trusting. Keep moving.

Divine Fashioner of My Destiny: I know that the plans you have for me are for my good. I know they are meant to help me and not to harm me. Remind me of your promises as I go through seasons of trials and frustration.

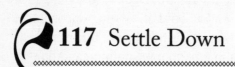

117 Settle Down

The Lord said, "Go out and stand on the mountain in the presence of the Lord, for the Lord is about to pass by." Then a great and powerful wind tore the mountains apart and shattered the rocks before the Lord, but the Lord was not in the wind. After the wind there was an earthquake, but the Lord was not in the earthquake. After the earthquake came a fire, but the Lord was not in the fire. And after the fire came a gentle whisper. When Elijah heard it, he pulled his cloak over his face and went out and stood at the mouth of the cave.

1 Kings 19:11-13 (NIV)

I found that in order to follow my destiny, I needed to cherish stillness and quiet moments. In these times, I felt the presence of God the most—not when I was moving and taking care of business, but when I was just still, thinking about all God had done and all God had promised. My quiet, ponderings refueled me and refocused me so that I could keep moving *on this journey. It is in the calm and still moments that I learned to lean and depend on God the most —and to enjoy the ride toward my destiny.*

I learned to forgo some of the noise and busy work to just be still and listen for the whisper.

The world is filled with a lot of hustle and bustle. We are always trying to check something off of our to-do list, often in an effort to meet our destiny. Busy-ness looks productive and has an alluring draw, but that is not Destiny. The quiet voice of your future tugs at you when you are still and in touch with the truth that you have a future and a purpose. Connect with Destiny's unobtrusive voice and listen.

If you've never practiced getting still, discover the benefits of finding your quiet place. Develop a regular practice of stillness so that you can be attuned to Destiny speaking to you. Get to a quiet place through prayer or meditation. In that time of stillness, reflect on events and conversations that may be opportunities to move to another level.

Destiny Crafter: Create in me a desire to be still, a desire to listen for the quiet whisper of your voice. I want to be strengthened for the journey toward my destiny.

Mary's Destiny Steps

Set aside ten minutes today to be quiet and still.

Write out a promise from God, and post it in a place where you can see it often.

Spend time today replaying God's Word in order to counter the words of others.

Remember that you are a work in progress. Remind yourself today that God is molding you to fit into your destiny.

Walk forward boldly with the view you've been shown. It is enough for now.

Create a vision statement that affirms your destiny. Recite it each day as you embrace your destiny while journeying toward it.

The Journey: Beauty from Ashes

*The Spirit of the Sovereign LORD is on me, because the LORD has
anointed me to proclaim good news to the poor. He has sent me to
bind up the brokenhearted, to proclaim freedom for the captives
and release from darkness for the prisoners, to proclaim the year of
the LORD's favor and the day of vengeance of our God, to comfort all
who mourn, and provide for those who grieve in Zion—to bestow
on them a crown of beauty instead of ashes, the oil of joy instead of
mourning, and a garment of praise instead of a spirit of despair.
They will be called oaks of righteousness, a planting of the LORD for
the display of his splendor.*

*I delight greatly in the LORD; my soul rejoices in my God. For he
has clothed me with garments of salvation and arrayed me in a robe
of his righteousness, as a bridegroom adorns his head like a priest,
and as a bride adorns herself with her jewels. For as the soil makes
the sprout come up and a garden causes seeds to grow, so the Sovereign LORD will make righteousness and praise spring up before all
nations.*

Isaiah 61:1-3, 10-11 (NIV)

We have each journeyed before you, finding count-less adventures on the road to Destiny.

I (Tamar) took clever and bold steps.

I (Rahab) made a complete U-turn.

I (Ruth) broke cultural norms, traveled abroad, and found a new life.

I (Bathsheba) found my voice despite the scandal.

I (Mary) birthed the ultimate gift to humankind, your Savior and mine.

What destinies! What journeys! How will Destiny unfold for you? What will be said about your contribution to your fellow sisters and brothers?

What are you going to do with the life you have left? Find the courage to make Destiny choices for the time you have. Dream it. Believe it. Live it.

Creator of My Destiny: Grant me the courage to go after my destiny.